Contemporary Issues
in
American Education

Contemporary Issues
in
American Education

F. ROBERT PAULSEN, *Editor*

THE UNIVERSITY OF ARIZONA PRESS
Tucson

THE UNIVERSITY OF ARIZONA PRESS
TUCSON, ARIZONA

Copyright © 1967
The Arizona Board of Regents
Library of Congress Catalog
Card No. 66-24302.
Manufactured in the U.S.A.

TABLE OF CONTENTS

FOREWORD

THE PRESENTATIONS IN THIS PUBLICATION ARE FROM A SERIES OF LECTURES presented in the College of Education at the University of Arizona during 1965–66. As an on-going program considering contemporary issues of American education, the College of Education Colloquia have afforded an opportunity to bring visiting professors as well as resident faculty to the platform. There is both presentation to and dialogue with colleagues and students.

These papers do not represent any special or single theme. They may, therefore, be considered separately and without concern for sequence. Each paper does, however, represent a point of view relating to an important issue or circumstance confronting American education in the mid-twentieth century. The authors share a vast amount of experience. Their wisdom must be related to their ability to interpret the signs of the times and to project into the future those demands which the nation will make of the educational endeavor.

The editor's short contribution on the "Threshold of Being" sets the stage for several of the papers which follow. Although, as noted above, a sequence of presentations was not determined in the lecture series, most educators today recognize that many of the problems relating to the ultimate attainment of objectives must be resolved through an improved understanding of the nature of man. There seems no better place to start than at the moment the child emerges from infancy to an awareness of himself as distinct from the world about him.

It is hoped that these presentations are informative and most of all provocative. The editor's task has been minimal, and yet rewarding. The labor was one of interest, but certainly appreciation must be accorded to each author for papers well presented.

We especially appreciate the work of Mrs. Nancy Leach, who typed the final manuscript.

F. ROBERT PAULSEN

ABOUT THE AUTHORS

DR. RUTH STRANG, PROFESSOR EMERITUS OF TEACHERS COLLEGE, Columbia University, and Professor of Education and Director of the Reading Development Center at the University of Arizona, is known and respected by thousands of educators throughout the world. She is the author of over 35 volumes and 700 articles in the fields of reading, psychology, counseling, health, measurement, and group dynamics. Ruth Strang is a teacher's teacher and the great effect of her influence is noted near and far. In the consideration of "The Potentiality of Children," Dr. Strang affords additional insight into her philosophy of education.

Dr. Marie Hughes, Professor of Education at the University of Arizona, is known widely for her work in group dynamics, the analysis of "interaction" in the teaching process, and in helping teachers become cognizant of the creative capacities of children. Dr. Hughes has devoted most of her professional life to assignments in the Southwest, but serves on several regional and national panels on teacher education. In speaking of the "Dimensions of Creativity," Dr. Hughes has listed concisely those factors which may help the student understand the concept in relation to desired educational practice today.

Dr. Laurence D. Haskew, Vice Chancellor of the University of Texas, is well known as a professor, administrator, and public speaker. Serving for many years as Dean of the College of Education at Texas, his influence and leadership have been noted not only throughout the Southwest, but throughout the nation at large. Dr. Haskew has written and published standard textbooks in Secondary

3

Education. His contribution here concerns the "Challenges of Teaching," and he concludes that, contrary to what some people believe, teaching is an exciting profession.

Dr. J. Raymond Gerberich, Professor Emeritus of the University of Connecticut and former Executive Officer of the American Educational Research Association, was Visiting Professor at the University of Arizona during 1965–66. During his tenure at Connecticut, Dr. Gerberich was responsible for developing one of the most comprehensive statewide testing programs. His approach to the "Evaluation of Educational Change" has been practical, but nonetheless imaginative. Both theory of measurement and appropriate methodology are considered cornerstones in any attempt to evaluate innovations and educational change today.

Dr. John Chilcott holds his professorial assignment at the University of Arizona in both the Department of Anthropology and the College of Education. The study of anthropology is becoming essential for the educator. The anthropologist has found that in a study of "culture," the analysis of schools and the educative process provide new insights into the understanding of man, his aspirations, and his efforts to achieve. John Chilcott suggests that "anthropology presently fulfills in relation to the behavioral sciences the role formerly filled by philosophy in relation to all sciences."

Dr. T. Frank Saunders, Associate Professor of Education at the University of Arizona discusses "Originality in American Philosophy." Suggesting that "originality" is difficult to find, he maintains, along with others, that American pragmatism is a significant contribution to the philosophical domain. The works of Peirce, James, and Dewey are considered most important for those persons who study the development of educational philosophy in the twentieth century.

Dr. Floyd Miller, Commissioner of Education for the state of Nebraska, has served as visiting professor at several universities in the United States. As a prominent educational administrator, Dr. Miller notes that the national goal, so frequently enunciated in recent months, of a new level of excellence in American education points directly to the state education departments. Indeed, with every manifestation of increased educational leadership and financial support from the federal government, there must be a concomitant response in every state if the schools are to be improved and the youth of this country provided a better education.

Dr. Roald F. Campbell, Dean of the Graduate School of Education at the University of Chicago, is a noted scholar among American educators. He has served as a teacher, superintendent of schools, and college professor. He has also been Director of the Midwest Center for Administration at the University of Chicago. Dr. Campbell is the author of numerous books and articles on the administration of public education. Most recently, he has been concerned with analyzing the control of public education, particularly as this control might be viewed by the anthropologist, sociologist, and political scientist. Dr. Campbell insists, however, that we cannot reduce the means to resolve all of our societal problems to education alone. Those who control education must assume some responsibility for moving forward toward the Great Society, but those who control other societal institutions must likewise understand and help perpetuate the American set of values.

Dr. William J. Ellena, Associate Executive Secretary of the American Association of School Administrators, is widely known by educational administrators from Maine to California. In constant demand as a public speaker, Dr. Ellena travels extensively in the accomplishment of his assignments. Occasionally, he is inclined to prognosticate. The presentation of "Man and the Day After Tomorrow" might be considered prophetic by some persons. It is provocative when one considers possible demands to be made by the future society. Certainly, we agree that "it is time for school administrators to begin thinking unthinkable thoughts" as they plan for the educational programs required in the years to come.

Dr. F. Robert Paulsen, editor of this publication, is the Dean of the College of Education at the University of Arizona. Previously he served as a school administrator, professor, and Dean of the School of Education at the University of Connecticut.

F. ROBERT PAULSEN

THE THRESHOLD OF BEING

SEVERAL SITUATIONS IN OUR SOCIETY EMPHASIZE THE IMPORTANCE OF improving and developing educational programs for young children. The importance accorded to good social adjustment and to the ability to function effectively in a group has led to the concern for providing young children with opportunities for pre-school experiences. The expansion of kindergarten and nursery school programs has also been prompted by the need for better care of those children whose mothers have entered the labor force. Certainly, the school drop-out and the rising rate of juvenile delinquency have aroused interest in providing worthwhile experiences in the early years for the culturally deprived child. It must be noted, as well, that educators and many behavioral scientists now believe that any program which will stimulate the creative capacities of children will increase the chances for successful school work and the prospects for a productive life. In effect, there are many reasons apparent for extending schooling downward into those years wherein the child emerges from the infant.

In October, 1964, there were 3,187,000 children aged three to five years enrolled in public and private nursery schools and kindergartens in the United States.[1] We know that "headstart" projects initiated in the summer of 1965 have not had the impact on the development of early childhood educational programs it was assumed they would have. In October, 1965, a total of 3,407,000 children were engaged in these pre-school classes, not many more

[1]See: Samuel Schloss, "Enrollment of 3-, 4-, and 5-Year-Olds in Nursery Schools and Kindergartens: October, 1964," Washington, D.C.: U.S. Department of Health, Education & Welfare, June, 1965.

7

than in the preceding year.[2] Nevertheless, early childhood education is being discussed and promoted more and more, and it is believed that eventually both kindergartens and nursery schools will develop in most American communities.

We are not concerned here primarily with problems relating to pre-school children. Rather, our task is to consider several ideas and a philosophy of education which relate to the concept of "being," and to the achievement of self-identity and self-fulfillment as primary goals of education.

SEARCH FOR SELF

During the past decade, anthropologists, educators, and psychologists have manifested a growing interest in the analysis of and need for understanding the concept of "self." Piaget and others have suggested that in the beginning the child cannot distinguish between self and world. The distinction between self and not-self is built up slowly and continually. The very possibility of conceptualizing the self as a distinct entity is the result of many different types of experiences.[3] The "self" is the totality or composite of thoughts, feelings, and physical factors which constitutes a person's awareness of his individual existence.[4] In the consideration of "self-hood" great emphasis has been placed on the affective behavior or emotional component of the individual. This is not to ignore either the intellectual or physical aspects of the human being, but rather to note that one's ability to focus on emotion-arousing events seems to have some relationship to the development of a more complete self-concept.[5] A survey of the history of education reveals that "emotion" has been ignored generally in any analysis of what it means to be the educated man or even the human being. Only in recent years has emotional well-being been considered an important factor respecting educational achievement. Indeed, only in the past few years has emotional maturity been recognized as a significant criterion in the attainment and evaluation of success in many aspects of life. The emotional component of self-hood must be incorporated into any purposive concept of life.

Among others, Samuel McLaughlin sounded one note for educators to consider:

[2]*Personal Correspondence*: Samuel Schloss, U.S. Office of Education, Department of Health, Education & Welfare, April 18, 1966.

[3]See: Leo Schneiderman, "Repression, Anxiety, and the Self," in *Identity and Anxiety,* edited by Maurice Stein, *et al.,* New York: The Free Press, p. 160.

[4]See: F. Robert Paulsen, "Man's Search for Self," *Social Work,* July,1963, p. 114.

[5]Schneiderman, *op. cit.,* p. 160.

The human being is now viewed as an organism of purpose and meaning. His actions, to a large extent, are controlled by his purposes that emanate from the way he perceives his world and himself. The degree of self-esteem and the sense of adequacy a child has determine to a large degree the effectiveness with which he learns. Nothing is more basic to success than the building of self-esteem. Any practice which causes a child to doubt himself is tragic.[6]

R. Van Allen, coordinator of the Headstart programs administered by the University of Arizona in 1965, concluded his assignment suggesting that we must raise the level of sensitivity and caring for each child. Only in this way will the "self" be achieved and the road to self-fulfillment be made more secure. Allen wrote:

. . . experience has led some to realize anew that learning results from an *outpouring* of the child's ideas and feelings more than from the *pouring in* of the ideas and language of others.[7]

And, we would agree with Juan Mantoyani, when he wrote that any child might say:

I have come to fulfill myself—to live. Incapable of providing for myself, I need to saturate my life with values and spirit, to humanize myself. I should mature in a progressive relationship with my fellow creatures, with history, and with the cultural heritage. For this I need to feel the presence of a teacher. I need your spirit and not your hands. I am not wax that can be molded capriciously nor a vacuum that should be filled. I deliver my budding spirit and the plasticity of my being to the continuous play of influences and stimuli, to the protection of your formed spirit, and to the suggestions of the values which constitute the highest human state of being. I represent an uncertain destiny which should be encouraged to fulfill itself, an undetermined will which ought to follow the moral path. Do not oppress me harshly nor abandon me.[8]

PATHWAYS TO IDENTITY

Identity in childhood and throughout life is influenced significantly by school experience. If the parents have a strong orientation toward family organization, naturally the child's first identity will be with the family. The child may identify with a church group next, but we know that many children today are not afforded a sustained relationship with any organized religion. Identity with and through the school soon becomes of paramount importance to most children.

[6]"A Dynamic Child Discovered," *Utah Educational Review,* September, 1960.
[7]"Sensitivity and Caring," *Childhood Education,* December, 1965, p. 205.
[8]"La Education," *Phi Delta Kappan,* April, 1958, p. 316.

The greatest anticipation in the life of a child age five going on six is for the day he will enter school. The enthusiasm generated for such an experience has seldom been appreciated or utilized. Children should be given the most important opportunities to travel pathways to identity, and the first days and weeks of school should be a time never to be forgotten by the child nor passed by lightly by the teacher.

In the schools, children should be given their first real chances of defining to themselves and to the world what they might become as evidenced by skills, values, and goals learned and achieved. Although a child's conscious and unconscious self—what he is and what he feels he ought to be—may be largely fashioned in family identification, we also know that what a child learns, what he might do, and what he can become are now considered primary responsibilities of the school.

Certainly, identity comes first through the family, then perhaps through the church, but surely through the school. These institutions stamp permanent characteristics on each person, and if the experiences afforded have been positive and worthwhile, the various needs of the child will have been met.

If the child were sophisticated, he would know that his identity is being formulated by the teachers who guide him along each step of the way. How well the child will fare as he makes his way through the life-cycle in our complex civilization depends on whether teachers have encouraged the quest for learning, or whether they have caused children to become bored with school and afraid of life. In many ways, the teacher is the personification of reality for the child.

We know that even intellectual growth means much more than increasing competence in the academic content of the curriculum. Educators must stimulate in the child a quest for learning, an attitude of inquiry, a love of truth and beauty, a questioning and curious mind, and, most of all, a respect for himself. The learning of right answers is not enough. Children must be taken beyond answers. Children must be guided toward the discovery of answers —toward creative thinking, reasoning, judging, and understanding life itself.

From the moment of birth, the child lives with the prospects of achieving unique identity. There are many pathways to identity. Security, service, and success are psychologically necessary to the human being. In some ways these needs become pathways wherein one determines who and what he is. From the day a child enters school, the teachers must share the responsibility of affording each child the opportunity of finding both "self" and "identity." These are among the real objectives of education.

Parents and teachers must work together if the child is to be given the types of opportunities and experiences needed to achieve the identity of oneself. It must always be remembered that:

If a child lives with criticism he learns to condemn.

If a child lives with hostility he learns to fight.

If a child lives with fear he learns to be apprehensive.

If a child lives with pity he learns to feel sorry for himself.

If a child lives with jealousy he learns to hate.

If a child lives with encouragement he learns to be confident.

If a child lives with praise he learns to be appreciative.

If a child lives with acceptance he learns to love.

If a child lives with approval he learns to like himself.

If a child lives with recognition he learns to have a goal.

If a child lives with fairness he learns justice.

If a child lives with honesty he learns about truth.

If a child lives with friendliness he learns that the world is a good place in which to live.[9]

THE TASKS OF TEACHERS

Some years ago, when merit-rating projects were popular, many attempts were made to define specifically the various roles of teachers. It was noted that a teacher was a director of learning, a counselor, a professional person, an external representative of the school to the community, and a host of other things. Any survey of what teachers are called upon to do and what responsibilities must be assumed would suggest that any description of the "good teacher" must include his many tasks. In addition to the usual tasks listed, at least two more seem important: (1) To remain always a student of the human being, and (2) to develop a sensitivity to the needs of children, and in so doing to afford every evidence that as a teacher, he is concerned with and cares for each child in the classroom. If a teacher does not continue his own education and remain a student today, he cannot remain effective. And a teacher who is sensitive himself is also interested in developing this attribute in each child.

The teacher must try to assess as accurately and fully as possible how the child feels about himself. Only as a teacher understands a child's feelings does he know what is being learned. "Teachers sensitive to children as personalities place little stock in direct

[9]Author unknown.

teaching. They feel that it is worth the effort to make adjustments hour by hour when they contemplate the possibilities of unique growth of personality and distinctive social development."[10] Only in adopting a philosophy of education which promotes the importance and uniqueness of the human being does a teacher, as a person in his own right, fulfill his own destiny. Earl C. Kelly has elaborated on this proposition:

1. Human beings are the most important things in the world.

2. Children are people.

3. Each person is unique.

4. When any human being is lost or diminished, everybody loses.

5. Children are all right when we get them.

6. Every human being can change and change for the better as long as he lives.

7. No one of any age does anything with determination and verve without being involved in it.

8. How a person feels is more important than what he knows.

9. Freedom is a requirement for humanness.

10. Our task is to build better people.[11]

Nature has not been equally lavish with her endowments, but each person has great potential in terms of self-achievement and individual success. As educators, we must be aware of the potentiality of children and recognize the need to help children step through the threshold of being. In such a way, teachers manifest concern for the improvement of humanity at large. Teachers have the power and ability to provide those challenging experiences which children need to become happy, productive, and effective persons. Teachers can endeavor always to create a climate wherein children can learn what it means to live the good life.

Success may not be as difficult to attain as many would have us believe.

> "All things we desire
> And strive so hard to reach
> Lie freshly, like blossoms, furled
> In the heart of the child we teach."[12]

---

[10]Allen, *op. cit.*, p. 207.

[11]See Earl Kelly, *Prevention of Failure* (Washington, D.C.: Dept. of Elementary-Kindergarten-Nursery Education, National Education Assn., 1965).

[12]Author unknown.

RUTH STRANG

THE POTENTIALITY OF CHILDREN

WHEN ASKED TO LIST THE GIFTED CHILDREN IN HER CLASS, A YOUNG teacher said, "All my children are gifted." Like some of our most famous philosophers, psychologists, and educators, this teacher was expressing faith in children's potentialities. Emerson expressed this faith during his life, and Howard Mumford Jones in a lecture given at the University of Arizona said, "Freedom is the power of man to realize the possibilities of his being." He urged a revival of belief in man's powers and potentialities. Among psychologists, Gordon W. Allport, in his book entitled *Becoming*,[1] described living as the striving to be and to become. John W. Gardner expressed the same basic idea: "For the self-renewing man the development of his own potentialities and the process of self-discovery never end."[2] Most recently, J. Donald Adams, for forty years contributor to and editor of the *New York Times Book Review*, deplored the despondency about the human condition that is reflected in the bulk of our current fiction and drama. While admitting man's emotional and rational immaturity, Adams noted that man occasionally "rises spiritually, as well as physically, to incredible heights. His potentialities are so great that one feels ashamed, as I sometimes do, for having lost so much of my faith in him."[3]

[1]Gordon W. Allport, *Becoming,* New Haven: Yale University Press, 1955.
[2]John W. Gardner, *Self-renewal: The Individual and the Innovative Society,* New York: Harper and Row, 1964, p. 10.
[3]J. Donald Adams, "Does Anyone Know What Creative Writing Is?" *Saturday Review*, September 18, 1965, p. 25.

13

WHAT BASIS DO WE HAVE FOR OPTIMISM?

All education is based on the assumption that children can develop their potentialities—that people can change. If there were indeed a kind of environmental predestination by which the nature of the child's future development were determined in the first two or three years of life, then subsequent education could not hope to affect him materially.

While fully recognizing the importance of the early years, we maintain that possibilities for growth are present throughout life. The very instability of adolescence is an opportunity rather than a calamity; it is a time when the teen-ager can put away childish things and develop new attitudes and more mature ways of behaving. When Dr. William Menninger was asked at a mental hygiene forum if early childhood experiences determined an individual's subsequent behavior, he replied that people can change—even after they are married. In the University of California's developmental guidance study, conducted over a period of thirty years, Jean Walker McFarlane reports that prediction is poor at adolescence, even when it is based on extensive data. For example, as an adolescent one girl was delinquent and subject to violent emotional disturbance; at thirty she was happily married and an excellent mother to her two children.

We know of many persons who developed their potentialities despite severe handicaps. Helen Keller immediately comes to mind. Ben Hogan became a champion golfer despite severe physical limitations. Helen Keller reminds us also of

"Milton, the blind, who looked on Paradise.
Beethoven, deaf, who heard great melodies."

Both transcended specific limitations to their talents.

During the war years we heard much about physically handicapped persons who developed their vocational potentialities when given the incentive and opportunity to do so.

When a child's deficiencies are severe, they are readily recognized. Such a child is likely to be enrolled in special education programs. But children whose defects are marginal and obscure may be misunderstood and subjected to undue pressures that cause emotional conflicts, withdrawal, or aggression. These interjacent children, as they have recently been called, are "among the most perplexed and perplexing of children"[4] to the classroom teacher. At

[4]Edgar A. Doll, *Education and the Interjacent Child,* Haverford, Pa.: The Vanguard School, January 30, 1965, unpaged.

the Vanguard School the potentialities of children whose disabilities are obscurely marginal are being explored. The staff is developing new procedures and new materials of instruction in order to make the interjacent child "an asset instead of a liability, the hope instead of the despair of his family and the public schools."

Our task is not to ignore but to understand mental and physical limitations, to obtain an accurate appraisal of the potentialities of children with such limitations, and to create in them a confidence that they can accomplish something. Many of them have been expected to do things that are beyond their present ability. They have become frustrated, emotionally disturbed, hostile, or withdrawn—not as a result of their limitations *per se*, but because their limitations have not been recognized, their strengths developed, and their weaknesses mitigated by skillful instruction and practice. Potentialities are not developed by physical maturation alone—or by the simple passage of time. For example, certain abilities essential to success in reading—such as visual and auditory perception—do not improve spontaneously; they develop only with carefully guided practice.

Potentialities are latent powers or abilities. Under favorable conditions, they develop rapidly during the first years of life, and more gradually and intermittently throughout life—providing that the individual's circumstances permit him to use his abilities or capacities. Children possess many kinds of potentialities—physical, intellectual, educational, vocational, social, emotional, spiritual. All of these are interrelated and interdependent.

HEALTH AND PHYSICAL POTENTIALITIES

Under favorable conditions each child will attain the best health possible for him. In the area of health potentiality, the relation between heredity and environment is most evident. It has been clearly stated by Craig and Everett:

Each child is born with individual and unique potentialities for healthy growth and development depending upon his hereditary pattern. Body stature, facial features, eye and hair color—these and other distinguishing characteristics are given each child at birth and become more apparent as he grows . . . Recent studies of children's growth corroborate much previous knowledge on the individuality of the rate of growth and the fact that children do not grow alike.[5]

[5]Marjorie L. Craig and Frances U. Everett, "Developing Health Potentialities," *Teachers College Record,* Vol. 61, May, 1960, pp. 430–31.

Each child has his own characteristic growth pattern; however, inadequate diet and other environmental conditions may prevent a child from realizing his optimal growth, physical fitness, and health potential.

The stories of many of the athletes who are chosen to compete in the Olympic games offer splendid illustrations of the development of physical potentialities. Although each sport demands certain hereditary prerequisites of body structure, whether or not an individual develops a high degree of proficiency depends upon the following conditions:

1. The child takes an early interest in the sport, which is recognized, and he is given opportunity for expression.

2. He receives expert instruction and ample opportunities for practice.

3. He is encouraged to persist and progress.

4. His particular talent is highly regarded in the community, and his successful performance is rewarded.

Under these conditions it has been noted that a large number of tennis champions were developed in a particular California community. Similar conditions are essential to the development of other special talents. Certain localities and certain periods of time have afforded conditions that produced some of our greatest artists, writers, and composers.

INTELLECTUAL POTENTIALITIES

Intellectual potentialities are "the product of endowment + growth + opportunity."[6] They, too, have a hereditary basis. You may have noticed that babies show marked differences in mental alertness almost as soon as they are born. One will be alert and curious. He will notice new sounds. He will reach out for nearby objects. Another will be slow to respond to any stimulus. Piaget described basic intelligence as a quality of mind that relates and organizes one's experiences.[7] A child who has this quality of mind learns more from any environment than a child who lacks it. Piaget goes on to say that "intelligence elaborates itself." That is, intelligence does not simply grow as the body grows. It is cumulative. The mind grows as it acquires "more and more complex and flexible schemata" (Piaget's term), and phrase sequences (Hebb), or what

[6]Philip E. Vernon, "Ability Factors and Environmental Influences," *American Psychologist*, Vol. 20, September, 1965, p. 723.
[7]Jean Piaget, *The Origins of Intelligence in Children*, New York: International University Press, 1952.

Miller, Galanter, and Pribram call plans which develop through interaction between the growing organism and its environment.[8] "They depend both upon environmental stimulation and on active exploration and experiment. . . . They are formed and organized by use."[9] The more intelligence is exercised, the more it grows. A high school boy expressed a similar idea—"the more reading, the more learning." Previously acquired knowledge serves as a motivation to learn more. Mastery of one developmental task makes it possible for the child to go on to the next.

Acquisition of the tools of learning augments the powers of the mind. Of greatest importance is the acquisition of language. Basil Bernstein, a London psychologist, has shown how the child's understanding of sentence structure helps to develop his view of the world and his ways of perceiving, thinking, reasoning, and remembering. His cognitive style is acquired from persons in his environment, usually his parents.

The child who hears nothing but short commands like "Don't touch those cookies," "Put on your shoes," or "Take off your coat," learns "not to reason why." For him the world is a place of simple actions; relativity does not enter in. On the other hand, suppose the child is accustomed to hear sentences that include a variety of nouns, activity verbs, and clauses that show relationships, such as "I will read to you as soon as I have washed the dishes," or "You may play out of doors while I am talking to Gran'ma." Such sentences introduce the child to cause and effect, to time and space relations, to a more mature way of perceiving and thinking. Language enables a child to use what the culture offers and to learn from more experienced people. Exploring and learning go on together in an environment that contains a wise person who can explain baffling things in a way that the child can understand.

The development of intelligence is influenced in still more subtle ways. In many homes, pre-school children's curiosity is squelched; they are unintentionally taught not to take initiative; they are led to expect failure. Dr. Robert Hess, Chairman of the University of Chicago's Committee on Human Development, is conducting an experiment to discover how mothers may unwittingly suppress curiosity, dampen interest, and cause the child to conceive of himself as a failure or a person who is unable to take initiative or meet unfamiliar situations. By tape recording the methods used by various mothers to teach a child a simple task such

[8]G. A. Miller, E. Galanter, and Kitt Pribram, *Plans and Structure of Behavior*, New York: Holt, 1960.

[9]Vernon, *op. cit.*, p. 727.

as putting together a jigsaw puzzle, Dr. Hess has been able to analyze the marked differences that exist in mother-child relation-ships. Many mothers in the lower socio-economic groups teach their children the same passive compliance that they were taught. In teaching the child to assemble the puzzle, they say, "Do it like I did." "Don't use that piece, use this one." "That's wrong; pick up this piece." In contrast, mothers from less impoverished back-grounds often use a different approach. They invite reasoning and encourage imagination. They say, "Is that piece the same shape as the space to be filled?" "Which of these pieces would fit in better?" "You found just the right piece that time." "What sort of thing would finish the picture?" In ways like these, mothers and other adults help children to learn patterns of thinking that they may employ all their lives.

Attitudes and feelings also play an important role. The child who has acquired a sense of trust is not afraid to venture into the unknown; he welcomes new experiences. The child who lacks con-fidence in himself is reluctant to risk failure again. According to both William James and Piaget, feeling is involved in thinking; there is always some affect in cognition, some cognition in affect. From our own experience we know that we resist being taught by a person whom we dislike, whereas we learn eagerly from a person toward whom we feel respect and affection. Children are the same way.

Intelligence, which is the totality of concepts and skills, of plans and techniques for coping with problems, "is channeled by family, cultural, and educational pressures."[10] Sometimes these pressures are too slight, as in a home where the parents are indif-ferent to education, or in a classroom where the teacher is "too easy" and expects less than the children can achieve. Sometimes the pressures are too severe, as in a home where ambitious parents are never satisfied with the child's efforts, or in a classroom where the less able learner cannot keep up with the more able children.

Intelligence tests measure actual rather than potential capac-ity. Intelligence may be better measured by "drawing samples of behavior for evidence of such organizational structures as schemata, operations, and concepts . . . than dimensionalizing and scaling within a vast domain of human functioning."[11] Unpredictable changes in individual functioning will occur under unspecified

[10] *Ibid.*, p. 729.

[11] Martin Hamburger, "Measurement Issues in the Counseling of the Culturally Disadvantaged," *Proceedings of the 1964 Invitation Conference on Testing Problems,* Princeton, N. J.: Educational Testing Service, 1965, p. 74.

future conditions. Unless we can specify the conditions under which the individual will live, we cannot predict with precision his future characteristics. Accordingly "the measurement should be used 'to improve status,' as Ebel suggests, rather than 'to determine status.'"[12] "With the seriously disadvantaged, diagnosis and treatment are infinitely more important than the misplaced emphasis on testing and prediction."[13]

We must distinguish between an individual's true potential development trend, as Willard Olson describes it, and a growth curve that has been deflected by either deprivation or overstimulation. Environmental stimulation may cause a temporary spurt in growth, which subsides when the stimulation ceases. Perhaps this is what happened with Dr. David Weikart's prescool children—although he offers another explanation.[14] These three-year-olds from disadvantaged homes showed a sharp rise in average IQ as a result of their experience in the experimental nursery. When they were four, they achieved still higher IQs, although the rise was not so great. But when they entered kindergarten at five, their scores declined slightly. Both Dr. Weikart and Dr. Deutsch feel that it may be unrealistic to place too much faith in preschool education as a "cure-all for the psychological problems of poverty."

Nevertheless, children's mental functions develop in the process of learning. Though it depends initially upon endowment, the child's intellectual potential develops as he acquires more advanced patterns of knowledge, more sophisticated thinking skills, and a desire to use them in a wide variety of new situations.

SOCIAL POTENTIALITIES

The influence of heredity is far less evident in the area of social potentialities. At birth some babies show more physical attractiveness than others. Some babies smile naturally; from the beginning they evoke smiles and approval. During the pre-school years, too, some children seem to have natural social gifts: they are sensitive to situations and to the feelings of other people. Verbal ability may help them to handle social situations easily. However, their subsequent social development is markedly conditioned by their subsequent experiences with people.

---

[12] *Ibid.*, p. 75.

[13] *Ibid.*, p. 76.

[14] David Weikart quoted in Bernard Asbell, "Six Years Is Too Late," *Redbook*, Vol. 126, September, 1965, p. 126.

The role of the environment in the development of children's social potentialities is vividly illustrated by a case involving identical twins that Barbara Burks once described to me. Dr. Burks interviewed and tested these twin girls at twelve years of age. They were practically identical on intelligence and achievement tests, and also similar on the Rorschach inkblot test. In the interview both were exceedingly shy. Each held out a limp little hand, looked away, and murmured an almost inaudible "Hello."

At this time these identical twins were placed in different foster homes. One of the twins was brought up in a comfortable home where there were many visitors. The family enjoyed one another and participated in social activities together. The foster parents were fond of the girl and gave her all the advantages they would have given to a child of their own. In her school, too, the teachers and deans helped the students to overcome their shyness and encouraged them to participate in extra class activities. The other twin was placed in a very different kind of home. The parents had few friends; they engaged in few social activities. They had a child of their own to whom they gave privileges and advantages that they withheld from the foster child. In her school, too, this twin was given little opportunity to overcome her shyness and develop social competence. The two homes, and schools, presented extremely different social environments.

About five years later Dr. Burks interviewed and tested the twins again. On comparable intelligence and achievement tests, their scores were again practically identical. They also presented the same Rorschach personality structure. In social behavior, however, they were extremely different. The twin who had been deprived of social stimulation and social opportunities presented practically the same picture as she had at twelve years of age. She held out a limp hand, looked away, and made no further contact with the interviewer. However, the other twin was friendly, poised, and socially responsive. She had developed her social potentialities even though, as the Rorschach suggested, her basic personality structure had not materially changed.

During adolescence the development of social potentialities is greatly influenced by the peer group. Youngsters who do not conform soon become isolates. Some retreat into a world of fantasy in which they imagine they are socially successful. This makes it still more difficult for them to face the real world. Others openly express their hostility and resentment. A few calmly set goals for themselves that are more mature than those of the group. Many have

"not resolved their conflicting desires to develop their unique potentialities, and at the same time to conform to the demands of the
group."[15]

EDUCATIONAL POTENTIALITIES

Practically all students have educational potentialities. No
matter what their initial achievement, they can improve. For example, we have much evidence that students can increase their reading
ability if they are given effective instruction. Students on all levels
of intelligence and initial achievement have made observable progress. Even retarded teen-age students with intelligence quotients
as low as 50 have the potentiality to acquire sufficient reading
ability to meet life's demands. An adolescent boy whose IQ measured 48, 52, and 54 on three individual intelligence tests administered by competent psychologists had not learned to read at fifteen
years of age. At that point he was given intensive instruction in
reading. He began by learning to read signs and directions that were
common in his environment, such as *Stop, Go, Exit,* and *Right Turn.*
In this way he built up a sight vocabulary of about 500 words. With
additional instruction and practice in phonics and other word-
recognition skills, he acquired in three years a reading ability equal
to that normally acquired by children at the end of the third grade.
With this functional reading ability he got and held a job during a
depression when many college graduates were out of work.

In school we are much concerned that pupils develop their
educational potentialities. There have been many research studies
of pupil underachievers. Underachievers are those who *can* achieve
up to expectation, but *don't.* We find a high proportion of under-
achievement among the gifted.

We glibly say that underachievers are not motivated, without
realizing how complex motivation is. We might arrange motives on
a continuum from the most pervasive to the most specific. At one
end would be the sort of situation that evokes the response of the
whole person. These situations are part of a system that influences
all of the individual's behavior. In this system a large part is played
by the self-concept, which is persistent and pervasive. Motives with
a more limited scope include long-term goals such as gaining admit-
tance to a particular college or vocation. Still more specific and
immediate are motives such as the desire to accomplish a given
task, win a certain reward, or attain a definite goal. Habit also plays

[15]Ruth Strang, *Helping Your Child Develop His Potentialities,* New York: E. P.
Dutton and Company, 1965, p. 208.

a part. Acquired knowledge motivates further learning. All these and other inner-directed goals contribute to the development of children's educational potential. In addition, certain situations exert particular appeals—what Kurt Lewin called positive and negative "teles"—that is, attractions and repulsions.

VOCATIONAL POTENTIALITIES

Educational potentialities are closely related to vocational potentialities. In fact, in view of the rapid changes that are taking place in the occupational world, the best way to prepare for future vocational opportunities may be to develop one's educational potentialities. Vocational guidance becomes more and more concerned with educational guidance.

Undereducated youth fall into the ranks of the unemployable. Today practically all kinds of work require at least the ability to read and write. Many unemployed young people cannot get a job because they lack training; they cannot get training because they cannot read.

Social development also plays an important role in vocational progress. It has been estimated that a large percentage of the persons who lose their jobs are discharged because they lack the ability to get along with people rather than because they lack specific job skills. With the enormous increase of service jobs, the development of social potentiality becomes still more essential.

EMOTIONAL POTENTIALITY

Emotional potentiality is more difficult to describe. It involves accepting one's self, maintaining constructive relationships with other persons, facting the realities of one's environment, and dealing with them actively and appropriately.[16]

Predispositions to emotional instability are to some extent hereditary. But under favorable environmental conditions the individual can handle even a fairly high degree of instability. The chemistry of the body may also play a role in emotional health.

A certain degree of order and stability in our environment contributes to the tranquility of our mind. Jerome Brunner remarked that "clutter is lethal."

[16]Marie Jahoda, *Current Conceptions of Positive Mental Health,* New York: Basic Books, 1958.

Interpersonal relationships exert a strong influence on emotional health. Children catch their anxieties, their fears, and their values from the persons who are important in their lives.

FAVORABLE CONDITIONS FOR THE DEVELOPMENT OF CHILDREN'S POTENTIALITIES

How can we help children to develop their potentialities? Certainly, we cannot begin too early. In infancy children develop a sense of trust in response to their mother's tender, loving care. During the early pre-school years, children begin to form lifetime habits of perceiving, thinking, reasoning, and remembering. It is during these years that they also develop equally important attitudes toward themselves and their world. This is why Dr. Hess and others have emphasized the importance of working with the parents of infants and young pre-school children.

In some homes children are encouraged to explore, to ask questions, to take initiative. In other homes they learn to do just what they are told, without questioning or understanding why. The element of timing is very important in giving help to a child. If a mother gives a child help before he needs it, she deprives him of the experience of success. If she waits too long, the child may experience defeat that intensifies his feeling of incompetency. We need to observe and understand not only what the child is doing, but also what the environment is doing to him.

During the later pre-school years, the child's early ways of thinking and feeling may be reinforced or modified. This is the assumption underlying the Headstart project, summer kindergartens, and other pre-school programs for children from disadvantaged homes. Many children from such homes have never known the "give and take" of family conversation. They seldom see people enjoying reading. In the pre-school groups they learn to respond to the teacher's frowns or smiles and to get along with other children. They are given interesting experiences and encouraged to talk about them. The teacher reads to them, thus acquainting them with the language of literature and stimulating their desire to read for themselves. They learn to look and listen. They acquire motor skills and eye-hand coordination. All these pre-reading experiences pave the way for success in beginning reading.

During the school years, children acquire more of the tools and techniques of learning. If they are from non-English speaking homes, they receive intensive instruction in speaking, writing, and reading. All of these language skills should be combined into one process with each aspect reinforcing the others. For example, they learn to speak, with proper intonation, stress, and phrasing, a sentence that has personal significance for them—"Will you come to our party?" The teacher says it, the class repeats it, small groups and individuals repeat it as they would say it to the children whom they are inviting. By writing the invitation while they repeat it to themselves, they strengthen the association between sound and written symbol. Reading what they have just written then becomes an easy and rewarding activity.

A successful curriculum is one that is based first of all on study of the children for whom it is intended. It takes into account the children's stage of development—their physical, social, emotional, and intellectual readiness—as well as the content that the particular culture considers important. Such a curriculum might be called a "diagnostic curriculum." It takes into account what individual children can learn and what they need to learn. School activities are self-rewarding if they are carried out with a minimum of failure and frustration. In a suitable sequence of learning experiences, success leads to further success. The child gradually acquires a store of interrelated association patterns or schemata. He fits new knowledge and skills into established patterns.

Communication skills become tools of intellectual and personality development. Through wide reading, the student meets numerous characters with whom he can identify. He feels with them. He sees how they solve personal and social problems similar to his own. He may get insights about why he behaves as he does and what motives lie beneath the surface of other people's behavior. This understanding may help him work out his own problems and meet his daily life situations with greater courage and acumen. Books that contribute to one's self-development are inherently satisfying. Reading thus becomes not only an expression of personality but also an enhancement of personality. High school students report that certain books have modified attitudes and points of view. The following comments were made by seniors:[17]

> Through reading the book, *The Grapes of Wrath,* I have received a better understanding of people who have had nothing all their life and end up in the world of emptiness and want. All my life I have had it pretty easy. I have never had to go without shoes, clothes, or food. So through reading this book I have gained a better understanding of unfortunate people who I never knew existed quite this way in our country today.

● ● ●

[17]Comments obtained by Mrs. Dianne Dawson Bailey of Palo Verde High School, Tucson, Arizona.

Before I had read the storybook about Helen Keller, I knew only vaguely about this woman's extraordinary courage and life. Because she is deaf and without sight, Miss Keller needed her courage to sustain and replenish what was left of her life. Her story impressed me to the point where I felt ridiculous. Ridiculous because here was Helen Keller, deprived of those things I am naturally blessed with, not stopping long enough to pity herself, and me, usually throwing in the towel the instant something goes wrong. She, a blind woman, has taught me to see my way to being a bit more courageous with my own life.

● ● ●

The book, *On the Beach,* was very good at showing what a terrible waste war is. I think if everybody read the book, and maybe *Fail Safe,* they would see how hard we must try to make this world free from the horrible threat of war.

● ● ●

When I read, *The Heart Is a Lonely Hunter,* I never knew how lonely anyone could feel as the mute did in this book. I know that a lot of us may have experiences of loneliness at some time in our lives but no one could ever feel as lonely as the mute did when he was left by his friend all alone to fight the world himself.

At all stages of the young person's growth—infancy, pre-school, the primary and intermediate grades, junior and senior high school, and college—we may contribute to the sequential development of his potentialities. If parents and teachers do their part, no child need later say, in Rabindranath Tagore's words, "The song I came to sing remains unsung."

Marie M. Hughes

DIMENSIONS OF CREATIVITY

Arnold Toynbee, has written: "In a human society at any time and place and at any stage of cultural development, there is presumably the same average percentage of potentially creative spirits. The question is always: Will this potentiality take effect?"[1] Whether a potentially creative minority is going to become an effectively creative one is, in every case, an open question. For Toynbee, the number of creative people are few. He writes, "The creative power planted in a minority of mankind has to do duty for all the marvelous physical assets that are built into every specimen of man's nonhuman fellow creatures."[2]

This point of view is held by many. A few people have something called creativeness; all others were left out when the "goodies" of inheritance were passed around. There are probably those among us who still believe that creativity comes directly from the supernatural, or believe the highly creative person is made, or is a genius. These people are sure that creativity cannot be studied or nurtured.

While we have many who believe in the rarity of the creative process, there are at the same time many others who are just as glib in pointing out that man uses only a small percentage of his brain, perhaps 10–15 percent. People in the United States are becoming more aware of the gigantic potential of man. And from Russia we have the announcement that a special institute similar to the one on the physical sciences has been set up to study ways in which man may attain the full use of his brain power.

[1]Arnold Toynbee, "Is America Neglecting Her Creative Minority?" in *Widening Horizons in Creativity,* Calvin Taylor, ed., New York: John S. Wiley, 1964, p. 3.
[2]*Ibid.,* p. 4.

A Russian psychologist writes: "If we were able to force our brain to work at only half its capacity, we could without any difficulty whatever, learn forty languages, memorize the large Soviet Encyclopedia from cover to cover, and complete the required courses in dozens of colleges."[3]

In the United States several books have been published expressing concern about unused human potential, and still others are in press. Moreover, we have a world that is *talent* hungry. A report of a United Nations commission points out that talented people from underdeveloped countries tend to move to the developed industrial countries. The need for developed minds is insatiable in viable industrialized, technological societies.

While we find one group believing in the scarcity, indeed rarity, of creative men and another group believing in the unlimited—at least for practical purposes—potential of man, it should be observed that these two points of view are not conflicting. Moreover, it has been indicated that the *world* is talent hungry.

Let us now consider the meaning of the word creativity and also indicate some of the directions in which schools need to move to foster the development of this aspect of human potential.

I believe all *normal* human beings are born with the capacity for human creativity. In other words, creativity is a trait of humanness probably distributed as other traits are. Furthermore, whatever the innate capacity of the human organism may be, it develops through interaction with its environment. An individual is always in the position of becoming. For example, man can learn to become aware of and respond to more aspects of his environment or become so habit bound that he cares less and less. He loses his delight in living. More recent research in geriatrics discloses the enormous role of emotions in the aging process.[4]

WHAT IS CREATIVITY

More than a hundred definitions of creativity have been compiled; a few samples here will suffice.

Drevdahl[5]
Creativity is the capacity of persons to produce compositions, products or ideas of any sort . . . essentially new or novel, and previously unknown

[3]L. L. Vasilieo, *Mysterious Phenomena of the Human Psyche,* New Hyde Park, N.Y.: University Books, 1965.

[4]D. Macmillan, Mental Health Services for the Aged—British Approach, *Canada's Mental Health Supplement # 29,* May, 1962.

[5]J. E. Drevdahl, "Factors of Importance for Creativity," *Journal of Clinical Psychology,* XII, 1956.

to the producer. It can be imaginative activity, or thought synthesis—not a mere summation. It may involve the forming of new patterns, transplanting of old patterns to new situations, the generation of new correlates. It must be purposeful and goal-directed. It may be artistic, literary, or scientific production or procedural and methodological in nature.

Harmon[6]
  The creative process is seen as any process by which something new—either a new form or new arrangement of old elements—is produced. A new combination must merit some criteria of logic or aesthetics or both, and it must contribute to a solution of a problem.

Provus[7]
  Creativity is that human activity which produces a self-generated solution to a new and pressing problem. The behavior must be new to the learner. "Arrangement meaningful in terms of goal-directed object" takes place in problem solving behavior.

Stein[8]
  Creativity may be defined as "that process which results in a 'novel' work that is accepted as tenable, useful, or satisfying by a group at some point in time."

These definitions have several elements in common:
  1) Elements are combined in new ways.
  2) There is a product—the behavior of the individual is largely goal-directed.
  3) Other people see the product as something additional and as useful.

There is some suggestion here that creativity defined largely as problem-solving is a culture-bound concept.[9] We might, therefore, add Milliard's definition which says simply that creativity is *personalized experience*[10] communicated in some form. This takes into consideration art, literature, drama, and perhaps music. It also adds to the concept the role of the uniquely inner experience of the individual.

  Carl Rogers summarizes an acceptable point of view: "the emergence in activities of a novel relational product, growing out

[6]L. R. Harmon, "Social and Technological Determinants of Creativity," in *1955 University of Utah, Research Conference on the Identification of Creative Scientific Talent,* C. W. Taylor, ed., Salt Lake City: University of Utah.

[7]Malcolm Provus, "Some Personal Observations on Creativity," in *Instructional Media and Creativity,* Calvin Taylor, ed., New York: John Wiley and Sons, 1966.

[8]Morris Stein, "Creativity and Culture," *Journal of Psychology,* Vol. XXXVI, 1953.

[9]Geraldine Joncich, "A Culture-Bound Concept of Creativity: A Social Historian's Culture, Centering on Recent Research Report," *Educational Theory,* Vol. XIV, 1964.

[10]Cecil Milliard, "The Development of Creative Ability," in *Child Growth and Development* (rev.), Boston: D. C. Heath & Co., 1958.

of the uniqueness of the individual on the one hand, and the materials, events, people, or circumstances of his life on the other."[11]

If all people possess creativity and if it is manifest in all phases of life's activities—a mother with her children, a man fixing his camp tent, a new symphony or the formulation of a theory of relativity—the question becomes how may we talk about these products in ways that are meaningful.

LEVELS OF CREATIVITY

A concept of levels of creativity appears necessary.

I. *Expressive Creativity*
   a) Independent expression where skills, originality, and quality of product are unimportant.
   b) Spontaneous creations of children.
   Perhaps basic to later creative production, this aspect of creativity is most frequently seen in children's drawings and dramatic plays.[12]

II. *Productive Creativity*
   a) In daily activities of housekeeping and food serving, the rearrangement of furniture, and the spontaneous use of a tool or dish for something other than that intended.
   b) In the achievement of a new level of proficiency, although the products may not be stylistically discernible from the products of others.
   c) In the development of techniques and the use of materials.

This level and the next are most recognized as a major aspect of American life.

III. *Inventive Creativity (boundary pushing)*
   a) Ingenuity with materials, techniques, and methods.
   b) Perception of new and unusual relationships.
   c) Perception of new uses of old parts.
   d) Ingenuity in use of tools, developing new ones, finding new uses for old ones.
   e) Ingenuity in symbolic interpretation of subject matter.

IV. *Innovative Creativity*
   When basic assumptions of a field are sufficiently under-

[11]Carl Rogers, "Toward a Theory of Creativity," in H. Anderson, *Creativity and Its Cultivation*, New York: Harper and Bros., 1959, Chapter VI.

[12]Irving Taylor, "The Nature of the Creative Process," *An Examination of the Creative Process*, Paul Smith, ed., New York: Hastings House, 1959.

stood so that improvement is possible, innovative creativity can occur.

For example, Jung and Adler left Freud to establish their own schools of psychology.

V. *Emergentive Creativity (boundary breaking)*

Creativity at the emergentive or boundary-breaking level requires the overthrow of an old assumption for *new* assumptions. Freud, Picasso, and Wright are examples. In science, Einstein stands predominant for actually stating new concepts of time and space.

This level of creativity is the most influential and the least common. It is, of course, the level about which least is known. Such creative people have tremendous capacity for abstracting and synthesizing—capacity to reorganize and visualize. The scope of their endeavor is usually very great.

It has been suggested that creativity of the highest sort "alters the universe of meaning by introducing into it some new element of meaning or some new order of significance." NASA scientists' ratings on creativity are given for the number of fields *affected* by the new discovery. For example, the concept of germs as a prime agency in illness affected more than one field of human endeavor. The widespread significance of the contribution of the highest products of the creative process need not obscure for us the meaning of lower levels of creativity to social and personal well-being.

UNDERSTANDING THE CREATIVE PROCESS

Complete understanding of the creative process presents great theoretical and methodological problems. A beginning has been made in the attempt to answer the question: How do creative individuals differ from less creative? In this case, creative individuals are designated as such by their peers, writers by other writers, architects by other architects, scientists by fellow scientists.

THE ATTRIBUTES OF CREATIVE INDIVIDUALS

The studies of scientists by Ann Roe and the seven-year study of the California Personnel Assessment Institute describe attributes of creative individuals.[13]

[13]Ann Roe, "A Psychological Study of Eminent Psychologists and Anthropologists and a Comparison with Biological and Physical Scientists," *Psychological Monographs,* Vol. 65, No. 14, 1953. Frank Barron, *Creativity and Psychological Health,* Princeton: Van Nostrand, 1963. Donald MacKinnon, "Creativity and Images of Self," in *The Study of Lives,* Robert White, ed., New York: Atherton, 1963.

First and foremost, creative individuals are psychodynamically complex. They are people who have more nearly achieved their biological potential. It has been said that the less-creative man accepts himself, but the creative man *re-makes* himself. This is a characteristic of great relevance when man lives with constant change and when new occupational skills must be learned several times during one's life.

A second characteristic is that of self-confidence. This appears in autonomous behavior and independence in judgment. Students in school often demonstrate these qualities in self-directed and self-initiated work. Although teachers may find these qualities somewhat uncomfortable, they are the qualities possessed by the more socially productive people of our society. It may be argued that independence and autonomy are also required for responsible citizenship since they are the qualities which serve as armor against the demagogue.

A third quality has been noted as that of courage or the ability to act on an educated guess. Any creative act by definition of being new makes the creator a minority of one, at least for a short period of time. In the material world, where our success is notable, a process or product is challenged with each change made. As we move up the ladder of levels of creativity, it takes even more courage to challenge an assumption or an entire theoretical framework.

A fourth quality is that of intelligence. As a group, creative people are more intelligent than the general population. However, two points must be made in relationship to intelligence as presently measured. One, the study of any group (scientists, architects) has demonstrated that within the group the range of normal intelligence may be found. In other words, among the members of the selected group of highly productive individuals will be some individuals with measured intelligence in the lower range of normal intelligence. Provus'[14] Chicago study of over a thousand middle-grade children found that 21 percent of them could be designated as superior problem solvers. Of this number, 30 percent had an intelligence quotient of less than 104.

A second point regarding the relationship of measured intelligence and creativity is that beyond a certain point (120) other qualities appear to be of greater significance than intelligence. This fact should begin to be reflected in the screening by public schools of those chosen as gifted for special classes.

[14]Provus, *op. cit.*

A contribution made by the research on creativity has been the building of additional intellectual tasks for testing purposes. These new tasks do disclose a group of superior individuals who were not always identified by the traditional tests.

A fifth quality of creative persons is the ability to look at a problem from various positions, to consider alternatives. A problem is frequently restated in new terms or as a *different* problem. Such people are flexible and open to experience. They take in more data from their environment. To do so they are able to rid themselves of old categories or a single set. It was Lord Chesterfield who said: "When you look at the back of a horse from a hayloft, it appears like a violin."

A sixth quality, which may be seen as a corollary of openness to the environment, is that of sensitivity to the environment. As Barron says, "the creative sees what others see, but he sees more than they see." Mark Van Doren calls such people noticers. He tells us that Shakespeare was the greatest noticer of all.

A seventh quality pertains to energy. The creative individual possesses more energy than the average person. Perhaps he has more energy available because he is more committed to and involved in his work.

Since the individual initiates much of the energy himself, the eighth quality of the creative person may be that of perseverence. In a word, tenacity can be considered such a criterion.

The ninth quality is that of imagination. Its role in creativity is quickly acknowledged although the process of its operation may not be understood. Through imagination the past and future may be envisioned. What does not exist can be brought into form. Imagination brings together the emotional and the intellectual aspects of man's nature. Imagination can provide relief for the humdrum, humor, and playfulness that relaxes, thus allowing greater perspective on oneself and the human condition.

Without imagination, recognition of consequences of alternative action, rehearsal for action, the planning and goal-directedness of many actions could not occur with present efficiency.

The pleasures derived from the imagination of artists—a Chagall, for example—or from inventors, such as the Wright brothers, cannot be assessed. Any underdevelopment of imagination lessens the human potential.

The tenth quality of the creative individual is the ability to tolerate ambiguity. This quality is related to the willingness to view a phenomenon in its complete complexity. To do this makes possible the consideration of a larger amount of data which should result in more effective decisions. When one must solve a problem immediately, it is almost necessary to solve it in the same old way within the same set. One who is open to experience is bound to live in a more complex world. The toleration of ambiguity allows one to build new systems of order. The more creative people appear to enjoy the process of bringing order out of the most ambiguous and complex situations.

In considering creativity, an eleventh quality should be mentioned; that is the characteristic of knowledgeableness, especially in one's own field. It is necessary to differentiate between the quantity of information one possesses and the manner in which he uses the information. Since much of creativity results from the combining of elements not hitherto brought together, it stands to reason that one must possess a great amount of information in his field of work. However, it requires more than the processing of discrete items of information. The creative individual can see relationships not sensed by others; moreover, he can make "leaps" that connect or transform things or ideas.

SCHOOL PROGRAMS

If the attributes or qualities described are related to creativity and the fulfillment of one's potential, then we must ask how school programs can cultivate personal confidence, fluency, flexibility, imagination, commitment, curiosity, openness, and so forth? What are the basic changes needed in school programs?

First, the schools could increase *perceptual* experience. Children are voracious consumers of their environment. How can we maintain this curiosity and interest? Needless to say, more time should be spent away from the enclosure that is the classroom. We might substitute trips into the community accompanied by conversations with people engaged in a variety of human activities. There should be return trips to note changes, and discussions with imagination to project what may follow certain types of change. In time, it may be possible to check one's projection of consequences.

Second, there must be greater use made of personal experiences —not only the concrete, subjective experiences, but the recall of what one has read or heard. There should be questions such as "Did this happen to you?" "How?" "When?" "What would you do if . . .?" "Have we read anything similar to this?" Teachers have yet to learn to utilize and integrate the "personal" so that it has relevance, yet this is one way new learning becomes meaningful;

moreover, it is a way in which the school can contribute to the efficient use of information. It helps to establish a way of thinking.

Third, we need to learn to value the ideas of children and the way they play with possibilities. Many of their ideas may seem silly, but discrimination evolves; it is not likely to be well developed in a fifth and sixth grader. Researchers have said that the best way to discover creative children in these grades is to ask for nominations of those who have the silliest ideas. The best ways to elicit and probe children's ideas have not been devised. This is a fertile field for research, one that will give us surprises and pay off well.

Fourth, teachers need to be more aware of self-directed and self-initiated work. Such work must be recognized and encouraged. It is out of such endeavors that *involvement* develops. Commitment usually follows involvement. Allied to self-direction is the need to introduce more occasions for *choice* on the part of students. Much of the reading beyond the primary grades should be the student's choice; this enables him to develop a sustained interest. Art work is another area wherein choice should be encouraged. And projects in science and social science could be greatly diversified to allow for individual preferences.

Fifth, teachers need to be aware of the repetition that leads to boredom. For many children the only excitement in school occurs from interaction with their peers. And this in a time when knowledge is increasing, concepts are changing, ideas are booming! Holt has written:

Give a child the kind of task he gets in school, whether he is afraid of it, or resists it, or is willing to do it, but is *bored* by doing it, he will do the task with only a small part of his attention, energy and intelligence, do it stupidly, even if correctly.[17]

He asks the question of us: "Why do so many bright children act with such extraordinary stupidity in school?"[18]

Plato stated that what a culture honors it will get. As educators we need to acquire a different concept of the productive student, and to do so we need also to reconsider the role of information and to view the teacher as more than an information giver. A field of knowledge *may be* envisioned as a territory, and knowing is not just knowing its items, but how they relate, how they compare with one another, and perhaps even more importantly, what pieces are missing.

[17]John Holt, *How Children Fail,* New York: Pitman Publishing Corporation, 1963, p. 157.
[18]*Ibid.,* p. 159.

If we are to educate for creativity and superior productivity then we must find ways to value students who:
- —handle more than one idea at a time
- —become involved and are in the process of developing their own meanings and preferences
- —exercise discipline in relation to the materials they are using
- —exercise their own judgment of what is important
- —demonstrate desire and ability to exercise their own initiative
- —exercise their imagination, be it playful, fanciful, logical, factual, or visual.

We can learn to value many levels and kinds of creativity—the originators and the elaborators; those superior in production or in interpersonal relationships; those who are able planners and decision makers and all who are necessary in carrying out the details of the most elaborate and original plan. As Garner Murphy has said: "We can learn to create and establish a habit of creating."

Perhaps after all a creative act may include much in our sensory world, in our cognitive world, in our affective world, and in our impulsive world. The creative person makes a single unified representation of these various facets of perception and indeed makes sense out of the universe itself.

Laurence D. Haskew

THE CHALLENGE OF TEACHING

At least two logical denotations are immediately apparent for the word "teaching." It can refer to the actual interchanges which do or could occur when teacher and student cross paths in the name of education. And it can refer to the profession of teaching as a career. The former is the meaning addressed in this paper.

It is necessary first, however, to place this referent—that is, the teaching act—in proper perspective. When one engages in the teaching profession in America today, he assumes responsibilities and engages in influential activities which extend far beyond conduct of the arts of instruction. For example, the combined teachers of this nation wield more power than any other structure in determining what is to be taught and what is to remain untaught. They sit in the seats of the mighty when objectives of education are selected and revised; they are much more than passive trustees for the goals of schooling in American society. With rapidly expanding conceptions of their roles and prerogatives, and with strong sanctions to enforce their conceptions, they move to shape details of the educational enterprise and to have a guaranteed part in its governance. In the final analysis, their vision will have definitive effect upon what man shall be in this century and what he shall reach for in the twenty-first century. These responsibilities and roles are not mere ancillaries of the essential nature of teaching; they *are* teaching. It is artificial to separate the acts of instruction, the interchanges which occur when teacher and student cross paths in the name of instruction, from this gestalt of being a teacher. But times have their imperatives. In our time, a new focus upon what happens

37

when teacher meets student is evident. This focus appears to be justified.

At a recent symposium in which Jean Piaget was participating, a member of the audience misquoted Jerome Bruner to have proclaimed that anything could be taught to a child at any time, and asked Professor Piaget to react to that statement. The patriarch's reply was long and involved, but his interpreter used one sentence which seemed to epitomize it: "The question of whether anything can be taught is never answered until two questions are answered— *by whom and how?*"

The teacher is always trying to be the who and to furnish the how. Success, even to a small degree, fuels the total undertaking of being a member of the teaching profession. Failure, while individually depressing, seems likewise to energize professional involvements. That is, the practice of the profession of teaching— multifaceted and complex as that total practice is—seems to revolve around the teaching act. Not everyone engaged in the teaching profession performs that act, and for many others it is a minor portion of the total workload assumed. But for nearly all, it is the basic *raison d'etre*.

The teaching act, as the term is used here, begins after somebody has decided that here is something a first grader, or a teenager, or a college senior can and should learn with profit, and a teacher can cause him to learn it. In this decision lies much of the fateful character of formal education and also much of the significance of the teaching profession itself. However, we shall separate that predetermination from the teaching act by defining the latter as what a teacher does to cause or expedite accomplishment of a given set of learnings.

The teaching act is performed by a classroom teacher but, under the present definition, not by that person exclusively nor even preponderantly. A teaching team may be the prime strategist for a teaching act, and execution of that act may enlist many individuals in personalized performances. Certainly, execution will also involve use of materials which, impersonal as they may be in form, constitute the vicarious presence of the wit and wisdom of those who produced the materials. This is a goodly company, these activists in teaching—instructors, writers, television directors, computer and other programmers, photographers, puppeteers, book designers, and scores of other teachers. Each has something he feels he must teach; each takes a medium and attempts to bend it to his end. This end is that some student, somewhere, at some chosen time will be caused to learn what the activist has to teach. Surround these teachers with thousands of other professionals dedicated to influencing the performance of the activists—supervisors, consultants, editors, psychologists, and media specialists, to name a few— and the judged significance of the teaching act emerges with convincing force.

It is necessary to qualify such judgment, however. The significance of the teaching act derives, in the long run, only from what it does to cause or expedite learning. Evidence continues to accumulate that the function of teaching and the function of learning are not completely dependent variables. The entire educational system of America may be excessively reliant upon teaching acts as *the* means to induce and guide acts of learning. Not only the exceptional, but also children within normal ranges, are shown to be disconcertingly adept in mastering difficult accomplishments without benefit of teaching acts, or—more to the point—apparently in spite of the actions to which they have been subjected. The inventors and promulgators of the "New Mathematics" were, remember, the recipients of teaching acts embedded in the "old mathematics." Students continue to learn, with miserably-written texts and treatises, with innocuous and shapeless lectures, and without benefit of even rudimentary teacher-contrived motivation—to illustrate from three recent studies. The point is that the teaching act may not be as crucial as the attention it gets seems to imply.

That act is crucial enough, however, to challenge the profession of teaching and every professional therein. It is a serious challenge. It is an exciting challenge.

It is serious because, to use a Biblical analogy, the new wine fermenting is tearing asunder the old wineskins already stretched to capacity. What must be comprehended within formal education in the decades now upon us is staggering in its proportions. What has been learned by only part of the population must, it appears, now be learned by practically all of a much larger population. What has been learned only partially—to use language for enlightenment, for example—has been of such benefit that we now demand it be mastered completely. "Acquaintance with" as a goal is being superseded by "managerial understanding of," adding a depth dimension to even the most elementary teaching acts. Every day of this perplexed age the knowledge of most worth is increasingly identified as being of the intangible variety ("ability to think," for example). This variety has been always a demonic bewilderment to the teaching act. And the wit who observed, "Of course college graduates today are more ignorant than they were forty years ago; there is so much more to be ignorant *of*," was documenting the plight of the teaching act. That act is confronted with overwhelming quantitative input. For it, the measure of a minute is how much learning of requisite quality can be caused to take place while the second hand circles once. It is evident that this measure must expand geometrically.

To be seriously challenged is not to be dismayed, however. The teaching act has responded with remarkable success—all things considered—to similar serious challenge over the last four decades in America. It is not unresponsive now. Neither is it unmodifiable nor forlorn. The glimpses already afforded of what can be or might be incline me to conclude that the serious challenge is simultaneously an exciting one. Four reasons for excitement may be noted:

First, the teaching act is essentially individualistic. Even the most sophisticated programmed teaching materials carry the stamp of individualism. Varied utilizations of those materials in instructor-developed teaching strategies likewise testify to free-wheeling individualism at work, often to the consternation of the program authors. Thus, we illustrate the great strength, and perhaps the greatest weakness, of the teaching act—its almost infinite adaptability to the genius of the one performing it. If the challenge with which the teaching act is confronted had to be met by discovery of the Holy Grail for teaching and by producing replicas of it for every teacher in America, seriousness would still be present but not excitement. Excitement comes from invention, creation, exploration, and just plain cultivation of individual prowess. Fortunately, advancement springs significantly from the same sources. The individualistic nature of the teaching act lends itself to both outcomes.

Individualism has other assets to offer. It permits specialization in those parts of the teaching act for which the performer has exceptional aptitude. As we gain increasing command of the logistic technology involved in team teaching, specialization should pay rich dividends. One of the most persistent sources of desuetude in the practice of teaching has been the expectation that every individual engaged in it should be a paragon of all virtues. This has never been possible. It is no longer even necessary.

Individualism likewise keeps personhood alive in a gargantuan mass enterprise. The teaching act is an impoverished and dangerous thing when stripped of personalities, of individualistic flavors and tones. Yet, that act is the preponderant definer of what it means for a young person to go to school. A great strength of the American system of schooling is that multiple, varied, and excruciatingly real personalities can play upon a student as he traverses the paths of knowledge. Our system still permits the teacher to get himself into the act, and it is from capitalizing upon such permission that personhood emerges—personhood for the teacher and personhood for the student.

The individualistic character of the teaching act is not all blessing, of course. The opportunity to be individualistically superb always opens up the opportunity to be uniquely dismal. Leeway to be inventive leaves room to be stupid. The teaching act is an intricate exercise with baffling complex ingredients. To expect to find two million persons who can perform it with what each can command as inherent wit, wisdom, and will is to risk futility for a high proportion of the American educational enterprise. The teaching act obviously needs more than individualism. It needs discipline, that is, guidance from without the individual in the same manner as the surgical act needs to be influenced by the discipline of surgery.

That conclusion leads to a second reason to be excited about the challenge to the teaching act. A discipline of teaching may well become a reality in this century. It has antecedents stretching back into antiquity; its immediate forebears are a mixture of folk wisdom, experiential testimony, and scientific inquiry coming to flower chiefly in our own lifetime. From these antecedents we have distilled a sort of homemade, impressionistic, and authority-dependent protocol for teaching acts. At points, this protocol was raised above the level of hearsay by genuine findings of empirical nature. At other points, it was raised to significance by ordering theory which, although soon demonstrably insufficient, provided rudimentary foundations for examining the teaching act and its outcomes. Chiefly, however, this protocol reflected an attempt to reproduce mechanically the masterworks created by gifted artists. Continually, the protocol was changing under the impact of discoveries made here, information extracted from there, hunches being played elsewhere, and advocacies mounted by prophets from everywhere. From all this has come increasing guidance for the teaching acts performed by two million persons. The individual teacher does not stand alone; he does have something to call on.

This something to call on is not yet, however, a discipline adequate for teaching. To say this is not to derogate what is available, but to indicate exciting challenge ahead. The communicable art-science of the teaching act is a far cry from what is desirable, but it is also a far cry from its beginnings. The most salient fact about it is not its inadequacy but its readiness to become more adequate in an immediate future.

For one thing, the teaching act is becoming the object of research scrutiny to a degree that is both startling and gratifying. Long held to minuscule reliance upon research endeavor because of lack of funds and lack of brainpower, teaching is now the recipient of more research dollars than it is prepared to digest. The private sector of the economy as well as the governmental sector is offering this opportunity to inquire.

Secondly, the teaching art is being progressively enlightened by great minds in other disciplines. Some of these minds are bringing their power to bear directly upon teaching as a major current preoccupation. More commonly, the constructs, concepts, and tools of inquiry formulated by savants in the sciences of man are being co-opted by professors and investigators trying to elucidate the process of instruction. This process of enlightenment by transmigration of knowledge and conceptualization has been a key ingredient in the evolution of a guiding discipline for the practice of medicine, of engineering, and of law. Its current aggrandisement in education holds exciting promise.

But even more exciting are the prospects for another operation essential to discipline-guided practice of any professional act. Regardless of the plea of intellectuals that an overarching theory is prerequisite to production of a discipline, the great professions have proceeded otherwise. They have created disciplines by the clinical syndrome. One element in the syndrome is an inquiring, careful, recording clinician in action. Another element is an arrangement for almost instantaneous broadcast to other clinicians of what was done, how it was done, and what the apparent results were. On top of this is a monitoring, synthesizing, disseminating mechanism which connects back to the practitioners as well as into repositories of clinical experience. This is a disheveled way to run a railroad, but it works. It requires what the profession of teaching, aided by government and private foundations, is just about ready to provide on modest scale at least. Networking interconnections are maturing rapidly; monitoring, synthesizing, and feed-out mechanisms are beyond the stage of infancy with promising indications that growth in number and stature will accelerate. Practice of the teaching act by inquiring, careful, recording clinicians is the element of the syndrome hardest to come by, but its manifestations in 1966 are exponentially greater than in 1956. One exciting part of the challenge of teaching in the next two decades is the opportunity offered to become a clinical contributor to the emergence of a discipline to guide the teaching act.

A third reason for excitement about the challenge to teaching is the burgeoning advancement in educational technology. The teaching act is going to be assisted in scores of ways by new materials, mechanical contrivances, different arrangements for grouping students and for student-operated individualization of instruction, school scheduling inventions, intelligent deployment of personnel, and new dimensions in conservation of time—to name only a few of the technological thrusts already apparent. The teaching act has been disconcertingly handicapped by the problem of communication. On the horizon one can see strong hints that this process will yield more of its secrets to intensive basic research now going forward, and some of its baffling characteristics may yet lend themselves to technical applications of research findings. Most of those who have essayed the teaching act testify that their greatest frustration has sprung from inability to kindle the fire of desire under the skins of learners. Again, there are grounds for belief that our limited understanding of motivation can soon be enlightened by the sciences of human behavior. Granting that direction of the teaching act will always be essentially an exercise in high art, not a slave to gadgets and nostrums, there is still cause for excitement in the prospect of being an artist whose reach and whose command of technique are multiplied by an almost limitless technological repertoire.

The fourth reason, and the final one to be treated here, for teachers to be excited by the challenge of the teaching act is the prospect for involvement in continuous intellectual outreach. Not since the early days of the Progressive Education movement has America seen so much attention concentrated on the teaching act itself as has been accorded it during the past five years. The current preoccupation has dimensions the earlier one did not exhibit— interest by the scientific industrial community, interest by federal government agencies, interest by those in higher education circles, extensive involvement by the research and development arms of major universities. All of this gives a strong indication that concern with the challenge of the teaching act itself may be pervasive and persuasive for a decade at least. This concern will provide powerful motivation for involvement by teachers in continuous education for themselves. If this education were destined to be a repetition of the so-called in-service education of the past decades, there would be little cause for excitement. In this author's judgment, one of the dark blots upon the escutcheon of the educational profession has been what it has put up with and has had foisted upon it as continuing professional education. But there are encouraging signs that this blot can be erased, that a new brand of intellectually grounded opportunities for professional growth is the offing. Such opportunities may not be plentiful soon, but the teacher who seeks them *can* find them. Certainly, the opportunity to be propelled into intellectual escalation must be a pleasing prospect for thousands of those who teach or who are about to enter teaching. The artisan role-definition for those who direct the teaching act will vanish slowly, but there is appealing invitation to help eclipse it.

Now to summarize. The challenge of teaching is to be found in large measure in the challenges to the teaching act. These latter appear to be crucial. They are serious, but they are simultaneously exciting. They are exciting because the essential challenge is to individuals; exciting because the individual, while standing on his own two feet as an independent creator, does not stand for himself alone.

J. RAYMOND GERBERICH

EVALUATING EDUCATIONAL CHANGE

CHANGE IN THE WORLD IN WHICH WE LIVE IS INEVITABLE. JOHN W. Gardner has pointed out that such crises as flood and famine, pestilence, war, competition from countries having superior technologies, and inner decay are all disruptive of the *status quo* and, therefore, necessitate change. He listed the ideas and exploratory studies of inquisitive minds as additional causes of change, frequently innovative change.[1] He also pointed out that a mature nation in its insistence upon order and system and in its unwillingness if not inability to look freshly at events tends to postpone change until catastrophe requires it, whereas a newer nation, loose in its organizational lines and variable in its policies, welcomes change.[2]

Three levels of change were distinguished by Edward T. Hall: in formal matters, where attitudes are tenaciously held and emotions are often involved; in informal situations where the boundaries are less precise and emotions are not likely to be aroused; and in technical affairs, where details of small consequence to the layman are involved.[3] The ways in which the concept of a mile is used can serve to illustrate this distinction. A mile, in the formal and usual sense, amounts to 5280 feet, whereas the term is used informally in the statement, "A miss is as good as a mile." Technically, however, a nautical mile, 6080.2 feet, and a statute mile, as previously described, have very different meanings and uses. Present

[1] *Self-Renewal: The Individual and the Innovative Society,* New York: Harper and Brothers, 1963, p. 28.
[2] *Ibid.,* p. 44.
[3] *The Silent Language,* Garden City, N. Y.: Doubleday, 1959, pp. 101–12.

45

resistance to the idea of substituting the kilometer for the statute mile illustrates the unwillingness of many persons to accept formal change, even though, in this case, the metric system seems to have major advantages over our hodgepodge of weights and measures—it is now used in about 90 percent of modern countries, it is already in use by many industries in the United States, and it is educationally simple and flexible.

A third idea concerning the nature of change came from Kurt Levin, who pointed out that the dynamics of effecting change consist of unfreezing the existing level, if necessary, moving to the new level, and freezing affairs on the new level.[4]

According to Jerome S. Bruner, as well as to many others, education is the fundamental method of bringing about social change. He reasoned that the school must reflect changes soon after they occur if the pupils are to be considered as living rather than as preparing for life, especially because of the rate at which change now occurs and the practically instantaneous reporting of important events. He also stated that ways must be found for feeding into the schools those new insights that are constantly being developed on the frontiers of knowledge.[5]

It seems appropriate to note that change comes about both *in* education and *through* education. Although the title of this paper seems to deal primarily with changes in education, I believe that changes can be made in the schools and in the educational system broadly conceived to provide greater encouragement for pupils to attain individually a degree of excellence, again to draw upon Gardner, commensurate with their respective talents.[6] It seems reasonable to think that this is one way by which change can occur *through* education as a process.

It is illuminating to note in this connection the relationship between level of education and the resistance to change disclosed by a recent Gallup Public Opinion Poll. This showed that: (1) College graduates more than twice as often as persons ending their formal education with high-school graduation (67 percent to 29 percent) reported knowing what the metric system is, and (2) among the persons who reported knowing what the metric system is, a similar ratio existed between the college and high-school groups (55 percent to 25 percent) favoring its adoption in America.[7]

[4]"Frontiers in Group Dynamics," *Human Relations,* 1:5–41, January, 1948.

[5]*On Knowing: Essays for the Left Hand,* Cambridge, Mass.: Harvard University Press, 1962, p. 125.

[6]John W. Gardner, *Excellence,* New York: Harper and Brothers, 1961, pp. 132–33.

[7]George Gallup, "Best-Informed Public Favors the Metric System," *Arizona Daily Star* (Tucson), October 17, 1965.

APPRAISAL OF EDUCATIONAL ACHIEVEMENT

Evaluation is a relatively new term in education, but measurement of pupil behavior has been feasible in the modern sense for approximately a half-century. In the measurement of pupil achievement the emphasis is strongly on his mastery of the subject matter, or content, of instruction, especially as evidenced in the most highly tangible and observable types of learning—knowledges and simple skills. On the other hand, the evaluation movement, which emerged in educational practice during the early 1930's, directs attention to the major objectives of instruction and the behavior pupils acquire in the process of trying to attain the desired outcomes. Consequently, the evaluator is concerned with the understandings and applications pupils develop quite directly and also with the attitudes, interests, and adjustments they form much less directly from school learning.

Achievement tests in the separate school subjects—reading, arithmetic, American history, and chemistry, for example—and coordinated batteries of achievement tests covering the major areas of instruction constitute the basic tools of measurement. Evaluation entails in addition the use of a wide variety of procedures and instruments, however. Among them are observations, interviews, questionnaires, rating scales, sociometric methods, and even, on occasion, the much-maligned personality inventories. It is apparent that two distinctive developments have occurred in parallel and interactively since the early 1940's. The first is represented by a change from predominant concern for specific types of subject-matter achievement in the classroom to concern also for various aspects of the personal and social adjustment of pupils. The second development is the new evaluative tools and techniques which make it possible to appraise the broad and comprehensive aspects of pupil behavior that extend so far beyond subject-matter mastery.[8]

Although major consideration of educational changes that have occurred or are in the process of occurring will be discussed later, one type of change that is closely related to, and is perhaps even an outgrowth of, the evaluation movement is directly pertinent here. Its major purpose is to supply some guidelines for users of evaluative techniques with pupils by distinguishing and describing types of behavior acquired in the process of learning. Educational aims stated in the form of objectives or purposes are too indefinite

---

[8]J. Wayne Wrightstone, "Evaluation," *Encyclopedia of Educational Research,* 2d ed., New York: MacMillan, 1950, p. 404.

and too far removed from the actualities of behavior to be very helpful. It is only when objectives are restated in the form of outcomes, sometimes called end-products of learning, that they become functional. The various types of learning outcomes can then be translated into the specific behaviors that are employed by evaluators in the construction of tests and evaluative techniques.

Outcomes of learning in behavioral terms were classified and characterized in two parallel but different ways in 1956. One, authored by the writer, classified outcomes into ten categories in terms of tangibility, ranging from highly tangible and easily measurable knowledges and skills to more complex concepts, understandings, and applications, and to such intangible tastes and preferences as are evidenced in appreciations, attitudes, and interests.[9] The other, a collaborative effort, dealt in the first handbook of two with such cognitive, or primarily intellectual, outcomes as knowledge, comprehension, application, analysis, synthesis, and evaluation.[10] Subsequently, the same group extended into the affective, or emotional, domain by publication of a second handbook.[11]

If the impression has so far been given that the pupil is the only subject of evaluative study, it is because the educational enterprise is operated for him and it is through his behavioral changes fundamentally that the worth of the system can be evaluated. Consequently, pupil success and improvement as appraised by such tests and procedures as have been discussed are often used as a basis for conclusions about the effectiveness of the instructional program. But the school can also be rated in terms of such factors as the quality of the educational program in subject and activity areas, qualifications and talents of teachers and other school personnel, and condition of the school building and grounds. Moreover, an evaluation of educational offerings can well involve such indirect but fundamental factors as expenditures per pupil enrolled, sources of financial support, and effort on the part of taxpayers to support education.

The child changes during his school career by growth in physical and mental characteristics as well as in the level and scope of his achievements. But physical growth to only a slight degree and

[9]J. Raymond Gerberich, *Specimen Objective Test Items: A Guide to Achievement Test Construction,* New York: Longmans, Green, 1956.

[10]Benjamin S. Bloom, *Taxonomy of Educational Objectives: The Classifications of Educational Goals,* Handbook I, *Cognitive Domain*, New York: Longmans, Green, 1956.

[11]David R. Krathwohl, Benjamin S. Bloom, and Bertram B. Masia, *Taxonomy of Educational Objectives: The Classification of Educational Goals,* Handbook II, *Affective Domain,* New York: David McKay Co., Inc., 1964.

mental growth only rather obliquely are dependent on education. For this reason, changes that quite clearly result from learning are of primary and almost sole concern here. Moreover, the methods that are most widely used in measuring and evaluating educational change are drawn largely from psychometrics, which includes educational measurement and evaluation. Therefore, the procedures that are applied to the appraisal of educational change, discussed in the next sections of this paper, are primarily psychological in conception.

MEASURING AND EVALUATING EDUCATIONAL CHANGE

One of the earliest and most perceptive statements on the measurement of educational change was made by E. L. Thorndike. In 1918, he wrote:

Education is concerned with changes in human beings: a change is a difference between two conditions: each of these conditions is known to us only by the products produced by it—things made, words spoken, acts performed, and the like. To measure any of these products means to define its amounts in some way so that competent persons will know how large it is, better than they would without measurement . . . will know how large it is, with some precision, and that this knowledge may be recorded and used.[12]

Unquestionably the best procedures for measuring change involve two or more comparable measures of the same individuals or institutions on at least two different occasions. Sometimes these are pre-treatment and post-treatment measures, as in experimental studies. Other times they are measurements taken before and after a time lapse that is considered likely to have brought about change in whatever characteristic or condition is under way. Consequently, it is the product rather than the process of change that is typically studied.

Evidence concerning the direction and degree of change is found by comparing the results obtained from two or more measures of status, i.e., of traits or conditions at a particular time. Studies conceived in this manner are called longitudinal, and they obviously must be extended over whatever period of time, often many months or even years, the person making the study considers desirable to allow for occurrence and measurement of change.

---

[12]Edward L. Thorndike, "The Nature, Purposes and General Methods of Measurement of Educational Products," *The Measurement of Educational Products*, Seventeenth Yearbook of the National Society for the Study of Education, Part II, Bloomington, Ill.: Public School Publishing Co., 1918, p. 16.

When longitudinal studies are not feasible, as, for example, in a case where the time span of a study would be greater than the life expectancy of the person who would like to make it, there are two rather common substitutes. One is a cross-sectional study of persons at different age or maturity levels as of a current date, based on the unjustified assumption that the older or more mature group evidences at a given time the same traits and characteristics the younger or less mature group will possess at a designated future time. The other is a "follow-back" study, in which historical records are used in obtaining information about a group of individuals currently under study.

The ability to evaluate educational change is prerequisite to success for all persons who take part in the educational enterprise at the professional level. As the "distance" of the educator from the classroom increases in terms of direct and continuous contacts with pupils, his need for and interest in the evaluation of change in pupils becomes more impersonal and generalized. This difference becomes apparent when consideration is given to the differing interests of the classroom teacher, the guidance director, the administrator, and the researcher.

A second approach to the evaluation of educational change, and one that cuts across and interacts with the first one, is the delineation of the breadth or scope of the evaluative study. The gradation of such studies can be stated in six levels: (1) Evaluation of an individual pupil; (2) Evaluation of a group of pupils; (3) Evaluation of a school or college; (4) Evaluation of a group of schools or colleges; (5) Evaluation of the educational system of a country; and (6) Evaluation of the educational systems of a group of countries.

Two types of gradations are included in this list. The first one, representing individuals, ranges from a single pupil to a single school to a single country; the second one, based on groups, varies from a group of pupils to a group of institutions to a group of countries. From the standpoint of differential psychology, major interest in evaluations of the individual, whether pupil, institution, or country, lies in the differences existing within the subject of study, whereas primary concern in evaluations of a group, either of pupils, institutions, or nations, is for differences between the entities constituting the groups. These differences at the level of groups are typically referred to as "between" differences. The "within" differences must be considered applicable only to the specific subject of study, or as a basis for ideographic laws of behavior, but the so-called "between" differences can in appropriate instances serve as the foundation for widely applicable, or nomothetic, behavioral laws.

In the ensuing discussion of measuring and evaluating educational change at these six levels, I shall review procedures ranging from those that can easily be used by the classroom teacher to some that are ordinarily the concern of educators in administrative and research positions. I shall also briefly consider the most pressing problems or difficulties that are typically encountered in the measurement of gains. However, the more specialized and highly technical aspects of measuring and evaluating change in education will not be treated in this paper.

Human Behavior

The individual pupil differs, within himself, in what are referred to as trait differences. He may be, for example, a tall, slender, eighth-grade boy who is a star player on the junior high school basketball team and whose aptitude and scholarship are at a higher level in mathematics and science than in English, to characterize him on a few of his hundred if not thousands of traits.

Classroom teachers inevitably and properly judge their pupils on the basis of observations, test scores, and other evaluative methods that have been discussed previously. But they often also have available supplementary profile charts on standardized tests by which a pupil's relative standing on the various parts or tests of the battery can be shown graphically. If different forms of the battery are administered annually or every other year, it is easily possible to represent a pupil's growth, or educational change, by adding the new evidence to that shown on a previously-used profile.

Another source of valuable information about pupil change that should be available to the classroom teacher is the cumulative records for his pupils. The records on course marks and standardized test results supply direct evidence on change in each pupil, and additional information on his development is sometimes provided in the form of anecdotal records and rating scales filled out by teachers in previous years.

Here for the first time there is a direct need for considering the reliability of scores that can appropriately be used in the measurement of change occurring over a period of time, or what are usually called gains. Measurement specialists long ago discarded the percentage score, still used by some teachers and by most civil service agencies in the attempt to measure achievement in such absolute manner as is represented by a "passing" score of 70. A desirable change will occur if and when the percentage mark is used only in relative terms, if indeed at all, in the measurement of achievement. Test scores and other numerical indices of educational attainments at best suffer from two deficiencies that physical scientists do not face, i.e., the absence of an absolute zero, since a zero score on a test has no definable meaning in absolute terms, and the fact that equal distances at different points in a score continuum are not truly equivalent. These problems arise in educational measurement whether the purpose is to measure the attainments of an individual pupil or a group of pupils.

Frederic M. Lord in discussing the second of these problems as applied to scores for individuals said that whether "score units are to be treated as 'equal' is sometimes made the subject of serious debate; . . . whether the units are called 'equal' or not neither adds to nor detracts from the meaning of the data."[13] He concluded that at present the matter is one that can be left to the momentary taste and convenience of each experimenter or interpreter.

Even so, the lack of a precise "yardstick" in educational measurement has long been recognized. It should be noted that a yardstick has both an absolute zero, or starting point, and equal units at all points throughout its length. One attempt to devise such a measure of growth was that by Stuart A. Courtis, who as early as 1929 proposed an isochron as "one per cent of the total time required for maturation" from a just recognizable amount to almost complete maturity.[14] The isochron has not been accepted by most measurement workers as an answer to the problems, however. Some deterrants to its wide adoption are probably the difficulty involved in locating either a zero point or an index of complete maturity in the learning of a school subject and the sheer complexity of progress in any course.

The lack of a more nearly ideal scale for measuring growth in achievement is reflected in two patterns recommended for use with individuals—one based on a technique similar to the time-series analyses used in econometrics and meteorology, and the other involving a Q-sort method of measuring individual behavior. The first is designed to gain "enough insight into the internal structure of the time-series to permit valid generalizations about the system's behavior" rather than merely to serve as a basis for approximate

[13]Frederic M. Lord, "Elementary Models for Measuring Change," in *Problems in Measuring Change*, Madison: University of Wisconsin Press, 1963, p. 31.

[14]Stuart A. Courtis, "Maturation Units for the Measurement of Growth," *School and Society*, 30:683–90, November 16, 1929.

predictions of the future.[15] Usual methods of graphing the results of a rather large number of sequential observations of a learner on a time scale are followed by quite technical procedures for using "correlograms" based on serial correlations in attempting to establish trends, oscillations around the trends, and types of sequential dependency in successive observations.

The second, again at a technical level, is a methodology of interest to the student of behavioral dynamics, the clinical psychologist, and such practitioners as guidance officers, who are often interested in studying the self-concepts of an individual or his personality as he is seen by others. Moreover, the technique most often used for this purpose, generally known as Q-methodology,[16] can be employed in evaluating such changes as occur in a single pupil over a period of time as a result, for example, of an intensive series of counseling sessions.

Methods of evaluating changes in an individual differ from those involved in the evaluation of changes in pupils in groups. However, many of the procedures for collecting basic information are quite similar, so the differences are primarily in the methods of analyzing and interpreting the basic data in such form that they can serve as a basis for careful scrutiny and evaluation.

Several major dilemmas complicate the measurement of change in groups when precise, as contrasted with approximate, evidence is sought. Bereiter listed three predicaments: (1) Whether to run the risk of overcorrecting or of undercorrecting for the spuriously high correlation that exists between initial scores and gain scores; (2) Whether to maximize validity at the expense of reliability in change scores or vice versa; and (3) Whether to treat change scores as if they were physical rather than psychological measures or to distinguish change in terms of value judgments that yield subjective and discontinuous scores.[17] He concluded on the basis of a rather involved analysis that the first dilemma can be resolved in large part by correcting for unreliability in initial scores and that the second dilemma is a false one because the meaningfulness of change scores does not depend on how well the initial and final tests measure the same traits. On the third and to him only real dilemma,

[15]Wayne H. Holtzman, "Statistical Models for the Study of Change in the Single Case," in *Problems in Measuring Change,* Madison: University of Wisconsin Press, 1963, p. 200.

[16]William Stephenson, *The Study of Behavior: Q-Technique and Its Methodology,* Chicago: University of Chicago Press, 1953, Chapter 11.

[17]Carl Bereiter, "Some Persisting Dilemmas in the Measurement of Change," in *Problems in Measuring Change,* Madison: University of Wisconsin Press, 1963, Chapter 1.

he chose the second possible solution, i.e., the meaningful scores that are subjectively derived from ratings of psychological change rather than the objective scores that lack meaning in terms appropriate to differential psychology.

Lord discussed two confusing factors involved in the measurement of change—the regression effect, and the influence of measurement errors.[18] The regression effect can be illustrated by the paradox that generally tall fathers are taller than their adult sons and that tall sons are taller than their fathers. However, the same pairs of fathers and sons are not involved in both comparisons. Lord illustrated the second confusing factor by noting that when we think we have matched two groups of individuals on intelligence what we have actually done is to match them on intelligence-plus-error, i.e., error of measurement. The same author elsewhere concluded that the simplest and best way to resolve these and other problems faced in the measurement of gains is simply to construct tests with high enough "ceilings" to measure pupils of superior ability and then to assume that gains in all parts of the scale are approximately equal.[19]

As has been noted, most of the theoretical problems encountered in the measurement of gains involve the effects of regression, of unequal score units, and of too low a "ceiling" in the tests. Diederich suggested that the provision by standardized achievement test makers of norms on gains when measured from different levels of initial scores would effect appreciable improvement.[20]

The techniques of measuring gains in achievement, apart from the theoretical problems that have been discussed, differ very little from those treated in many books on educational measurement and statistical methods. However, two recent publications deal specifically with the measurement of educational growth. To the book edited by Harris,[21] a number of chapter authors, in addition to Lord, Holtzman, and Bereiter, contributed treatments of such topics as univariate and multivariate analysis of variance, factor analysis, canonical models, image analysis, the P-technique, and the incremental R-technique. A chapter was devoted to the mea-

---

[18]Lord, *op. cit.,* Chapter 2.

[19]Frederic M. Lord, "Further Problems in the Measurement of Growth," *Educational and Psychological Measurement,* 18:437–51; Autumn 1958.

[20]Paul B. Diederich, "Pitfalls in the Measurement of Gains in Achievement," *School Review,* 64:59–63, February, 1956.

[21]Chester W. Harris, ed., *Problems in Measuring Change,* Madison: University of Wisconsin Press, 1963.

surement of gains, both for individuals and for groups, in a book by Davis.[22]

Schools and School Programs

Need exists for methods of evaluating the school as a whole and, less broadly, its program of instruction. The school staff and the parents and other taxpayers in a community are concerned with the results of school evaluation. School officials can safeguard themselves against the emotional and often unreasonable and even irrational attacks upon the school from some parents and other citizens by carrying out systematic evaluations on a rather regular schedule.

One of the most widely used sets of criteria for evaluating a school is that prepared for use in high schools by the National Study of Secondary School Evaluation.[23] A similar set of material is available for use in elementary-school evaluations.[24] Both procedures involve: (1) A preliminary self-evaluation by the school staff, based on extensive checklists and dependent ratings covering all aspects of the school and its various programs; and (2) A review of these ratings by a visiting committee of experienced educators, followed by the committee's report of its findings and suggestions. An attempt is made to evaluate each school in terms of a statement of its philosophy and objectives prepared by the staff rather than in terms of any arbitrary "standards" visiting committee members might deem appropriate.

After the checklists and dependent evaluations have been modified and approved by the visiting committee, a statistical summary of the evaluations and then an overall graphical representation of all evaluations are prepared. These results cover fifteen or so subject areas and four activity areas, plus the school plant, the staff and administration, and individual teachers. Provision for change and its evaluation is made by follow-up attempts of school staffs to effect improvement in areas of weakness and in scheduling reevaluations every few years.

Special programs of a school or college can also be evaluated by following up students who have completed or even withdrawn from the program through the application of relatively simple pro-

---

[22]Frederick B. Davis, *Educational Measurements and Their Interpretation,* Belmont, Calif.: Wadsworth, 1964, Chapter 10.

[23]National Study of Secondary School Evaluation, *Evaluative Criteria,* 1960 Edition, Washington, D. C.: The Study, 1960.

[24]James F. Baker, *Elementary Evaluative Criteria,* Boston: School of Education, Boston University, 1953.

cedures.[25] It is often easy for a high school to evaluate its college preparatory program in terms of the scholastic success and persistence of its graduates in college. Employment records of graduates and drop-outs, and supervisors' ratings of employed graduates of a commercial course, for example, are other follow-up possibilities for high schools.

Another aspect of institutional evaluation at the college level is represented by Pace's discussion of methods for studying the culture or environment of a college.[26] He described in detail a *College Characteristics Index*, consisting of 300 statements on various aspects of an institution's environment, to be responded to by the students. The instrument is designed for use in self-analysis by a collegiate institution.

Several standardized achievement test batteries now provide not only a profile chart for each pupil in a school, but also a profile chart for each grade. The grade profiles show how the average scores of the pupils compare with similarly obtained grade averages for pupils from schools that were used in standardizing the tests. It thereby becomes possible for administrators and researchers to compare the standing of the pupils in each grade with an appropriate norm. Such profiles typically present information for each grade in terms of percentile ranks, as on one widely used high-school battery.[27] Again, as was shown to be the case for pupil profiles, change can be represented by superimposing a profile for one year over that for a preceding year.

One of the most recent and potentially most significant long-range studies in the history of differential psychology is Project Talent. A major outcome sought is the classification of secondary schools by type—large or small, country or city—and by location in major regions of the country, in order to facilitate the development of more meaningful differential test norms than any now existing.[28]

Another purpose, related to a need discussed in a preceding section of this paper, is to provide a more accurate set of standards or "benchmarks" for authors to use in future standardization of

[25]Kenneth B. Henderson and John E. Georwitz, *How to Conduct the Follow-Up Study,* Illinois Secondary School Curriculum Program, Bulletin No. 11, Springfield, Ill.: Department of Public Instruction, 1950.

[26]C. Robert Pace, "Methods of Describing College Cultures," *Teachers College Record,* 63:267–77, January, 1962.

[27]*Iowa Tests of Educational Development,* Chicago: Science Research Associates, 1958.

[28]Project Talent Office, *The Tests of Project Talent,* Washington, D. C.: University of Pittsburgh Office, Bulletin No. 3, December, 1960, p. 5.

tests so that resulting scores will indicate comparable levels of ability. To illustrate, Project Talent reports that, "This may be roughly compared to the basic standards such as the marked bars for measuring length . . . which the National Bureau of Standards maintains."[29]

Project Talent involved ten hours of testing time in the spring of 1960 for each of nearly a half million pupils in more than thirteen hundred high schools located in all fifty states. About two thousand items of information, including thirty-seven test scores, were obtained for each pupil from freshmen to seniors in about a 5 percent sample of American secondary schools.

The graduates of each class group are to be followed up by questionnaires at intervals of one, five, ten, and twenty years after completion of high school. Results obtained by this procedure will be related in various ways to the items of personal information and test scores for each pupil, and also to the extensive data about the guidance program and the general characteristics of each school that were obtained by the use of lengthy questionnaires in 1960.

Public high schools have already been classified into seventeen groups on the basis of information of the types mentioned previously. It is expected that the differential norms on many standardized tests will in the future be based on these groupings and that each school will then be able to compare the achievements of its pupils with performances of pupils in quite similar types of high schools.[30]

National Educational Systems

Attention has recently been directed toward a previously unexplored area of educational status and change—the area at the national level. The school system of the United States has not yet been evaluated except by indirect and roundabout means or subjectively and often emotionally by its critics. There is need in education for an index or indicator of the quality of the American educational system that can be understood both by school people and laymen. Indices of this type that are regularly obtained on a nationwide basis and used in various significant ways are the Consumer Price Index and the Gross National Product Index.

An exploratory project designed for the assessment of educational progress in the United States was inaugurated about two

[29]Project Talent Office, *The Story of Project Talent,* Washington, D. C.: University of Pittsburgh Office, Bulletin No. 1, November, 1959, p. 8.

[30]John C. Flanagan and others, *Studies of the American High School,* Pittsburgh, Pa.: Project Talent Office, University of Pittsburgh, 1962 (lithoprinted), Chapter 4.

years ago under a grant from the Carnegie Corporation. The Chairman of the Exploratory Committee, Ralph W. Tyler, recently outlined the present status and future plans of the project.[31] He pointed out that it is designed to "report on the educational attainments of samples of children, youth, and adults," but that it will not provide scores for individual pupils or groups of pupils. Instead, it will present examples of what is learned by four age groups—nine, thirteen, seventeen, and adults—based on carefully chosen samples representing various geographic areas, socio-economic levels, and sizes of school communities in appropriate balance. Assessment instruments, now in the process of development in preliminary or "tryout" form, are intended to depict what all or most of the persons (upper 90 percent) are learning, what the average or middle individual is learning, and what only the most advanced participants (upper 10 percent) are learning. The assessment exercises are intended to differ from objective test items in some basically technical but easily understandable ways. No one person chosen in the assessment sample is expected to respond to more than a few exercises. No entire pupil groups, such as those in certain classrooms or in specific schools, are to be included in the sample. Consequently, no summaries by class or grade groups or by schools can be obtained.

Tyler ended his announcement of project plans by reporting that the initial tryout of most assessment instruments probably will not be made before the spring of 1966. He summarized the reasons underlying the project by observing, "We need comprehensive, dependable data about the progress of education in America. I am optimistic that we are on the road to getting increasingly helpful information."

Even though these specifications are intended to, and in fact seem to, distinguish this assessment project from a traditional testing program, Hand[32] and a number of others have expressed skepticism because of the fear that the outcome will be a national testing program.

To be discussed briefly here is an exploratory project that is almost certainly the first broadly conceived objective study in the area of comparative education. Cultural analysis has been the chief mode of inquiry, and anthropologists and sociologists have conducted a major share of such studies in the past. The study to be

[31]Ralph W. Tyler, "Assessing the Programs of Education," *Phi Delta Kappan,* Vol. 47, September, 1965, pp. 13–16.

[32]Harold C. Hand, "National Assessment Viewed as the Camel's Nose," *Phi Delta Kappan*, Vol. 47, September, 1965, pp. 8–13.

presented here does not in itself deal with educational change. Rather, it is the mere fact of its having been carried out that is indicative of a change, inasmuch as it employs empirical research methods in comparative education.

Tests of non-verbal aptitude and achievement tests in four major areas of education were administered about three years ago to samples of from 600 to 1000 representative thirteen-year-old pupils in the schools of twelve countries—the United States, England, Scotland, and nine nations on the European continent—in a project sponsored by UNESCO.[33] The tests were first constructed in English and French, with careful attention to the different cultures of the countries involved. After each test was tried out and revised, it was translated into six other languages—Finnish, German, Hebrew, Polish, Serbo-Croatian, and Swedish.

Results of the testing carried on in the twelve countries were analyzed more by comparing performances on the various tests within countries than between countries, since the validity of the cross-national findings would not justify such comparisons, and, even more basically, since no conclusions concerning differences among countries were desired or planned.

It was concluded by the authors that the results of this pilot study are little more than suggestive but that they support the belief that cross-national investigations can well lead to more significant results in the future.

Educational Changes

Having dealt at some length with methods for evaluating change in education, we may now turn rather briefly to the results of a few studies which had as their major purposes at least the measurement and sometimes the evaluation of changes. One exhaustive investigation merits first attention. Bloom analyzed a number of longitudinal studies of educational change in pupils, as evidenced by teachers' marks and by scores on general achievement test batteries, reading tests, and vocabulary tests, and organized his findings in the form of overall growth, or change, curves. A major conclusion relating to achievement was that by age six children typically have attained one-third of their age-eighteen development and that upon entrance to their 'teens they usually possess

---

[33]Arthur W. Foshay and others, *Educational Achievements of Thirteen-Year Olds in Twelve Countries*, International Studies in Education, Hamburg, Germany: UNESCO Institute for Education, 1962.

three-fourths of the maturity level they will reach five years later.[34] In summarizing his findings on change in human characteristics, including not only educational but also physical, mental, environmental, and attitudinal characteristics, he generalized that "change in many human characteristics becomes more difficult as the characteristics become more fully developed" and that the "amount of change possible is a declining function as the characteristics become increasingly stabilized."[35]

Three types of studies of educational change are now to be distinguished: (1) A few that were direct or at least indirect outgrowths of fairly recent military and psychological events; (2) Several that compared the past with the present or traditional with modern practices; and (3) Some very recent trends involving educational materials and practices.

Some Causes and Results

The first of two spectacular events in recent American history was the attack on Pearl Harbor on December 7, 1941. Momentous educational changes occurred in the American people between December 6 and December 8 of that year. There was a rapid and great shift by citizens of the United States toward the militaristic end of a peace-war or a pacifist-militarist scale of attitudes. It was accompanied by such forthright conduct on the part of thousands as enlistment in the armed services, acceptance of employment in plants producing materials of war, and in many other ways. These changes in attitudes and related conduct illustrate the effects of learning that grew out of this single, catastrophic event in America's history.

The second and more recent event was the Russian launching on October 4, 1957 of "Sputnik." Although the impact of this threat to the national security of the United States cannot be assessed completely at this time, at least a number of changes and trends to be noted in the concluding sections of this paper are commonly believed to be among the event's many results.

Two other causes of educational change were perceptive and forward-looking publications issued more than a half-century ago. They brought about gradual rather than sudden changes. The first began in 1897 when J. M. Rice, often called the "father of educational research," published the first of several articles dealing with

[34]Benjamin S. Bloom, *Stability and Change in Human Characteristics,* New York: Wiley, 1964, p. 110.
[35]*Ibid.,* pp. 229–30.

economy of time in education.[36] Under the title, "The Futility of the Spelling Grind," he carried out what was probably the first objective educational research study by giving spelling tests to 33,000 elementary-school pupils over a period of sixteen months. His detailed and perceptive analysis of results was the basis for his recommendation that only fifteen minutes of time should be spent daily on the teaching of spelling, because additional time does not result in better spelling on the part of pupils. This study and others by Rice contributed directly and significantly to the economy-of-time movement in education, and somewhat more indirectly to the stimulation of educational research and inquiry.

Another study that had considerable impact was the 1912 publication by Starch and Elliott that showed the essay examination to be quite unreliable.[37] Percentage marks, on the basis of 70 percent as a "passing" score, were assigned to identical copies of an English examination by 142 teachers of that subject. These marks ranged from 50 to 98. It is now recognized that these findings cannot be attributed entirely to deficiencies of the essay test, but they contributed to two changes—the wane of essay tests and rise of objective tests, on the one hand, and a shift away from percentages toward a five-point letter scale for final course marks, on the other.

Some Special Studies

A number of "then and now" studies have measured educational growth by comparing performances of pupils some years ago with more recent performances of essentially comparable pupils. In one of the most widely known studies of this type, Caldwell and Courtis compared achievement test results in the spring of 1919 for 12,000 unselected pupils from schools in various states with comparable results obtained in 1845 for 1251 quite highly selected pupils in the Boston schools.[38] Their major finding was that the 1919 children tended to make lower scores on the pure memory and abstract skills tests but higher scores on the thought or meaningful questions than did the 1845 pupils. Even though modern objective tests obviously were not used, the questions and scoring methods,

[36]"The Futility of the Spelling Grind," *Forum*, 23:163–72, 409–19, April and June, 1897.

[37]Daniel Starch and Edward C. Elliott, "Reliability of the Grading of High School Work in English," *School Review*, 20:442–57, September, 1912.

[38]Otis W. Caldwell and Stuart A. Courtis, *Then and Now in Education: 1845–1923*, Yonkers-on-Hudson, N. Y.: World Book Co., 1923.

presumably inspired by Horace Mann, were such that quite reliable and comparable scores were obtained for the two pupil groups.

The only other study of this type it is feasible to discuss here dealt with the manner in which American colleges awarded advanced standing to men entering, or returning to, college after World War I and to their counterparts after, or even during, World War II.[39] Colleges were so generous in awarding advanced standing in "blanket" terms to World War I veterans that many of them were unsuccessful in the advanced classes to which they were admitted. Returnees from World War II, however, were frequently awarded credit for military service, whether of general educational or special types and whether academically formalized or not, on the basis of their performances on the *General Educational Development* tests and special subject examinations of the U. S. Armed Forces Institute. Among the colleges and universities in which they enrolled it was commonly found that their scholastic success was superior to their own pre-induction performances, and to that of their male classmates who had not been in the armed services. Two studies of this sort were carried on at a teacher's college and a state university.[40]

One study and one series of studies worthy of brief note here compared pupils in traditional schools with those in experimental or progressive schools. Control and experimental pupils were matched on such factors as age, sex, aptitude test scores, and even socio-economic class in these studies. Chamberlin and his colleagues during the late 1930s followed into college the graduates of thirty experimental high schools and their control counterparts in validating the success of the Progressive Education Association member schools in preparing their graduates for college.[41] Wrightstone made three comparisons of pupils at the elementary-school and high-school levels who were attending traditional and experimental or newer schools.[42] Results of the four studies were very similar in

[39]Ralph W. Tyler, "Sound Credit for Military Experience," *Annals of the American Academy of Political and Social Science*, 231:58–64, January, 1944.

[40]Ernest L. Welborn, "The Scholarship of Veterans Attending a Teachers College," *Journal of Educational Research*, 40:209–14; November, 1946; Ronald B. Thompson and Marie A. Flesher, "Comparative Academic Records of Veterans and Civilian Students," *Journal of the American Association of Collegiate Registrars*, 22:176–79, January, 1947.

[41]Charles D. Chamberlin and others, *Did They Succeed In College?* New York: Harper and Brothers, 1942.

[42]J. Wayne Wrightstone, *Appraisal of New Practices in Selected Public Schools; Appraisal of Experimental High School Practices; Appraisal of Newer Elementary School Practices*, New York: Bureau of Publications, Teachers College, Columbia University, 1935, 1936, and 1938.

showing that pupils from the experimental and progressive schools were at least equal to pupils from the more traditional schools in acquisition of the fundamentals of learning and that they were superior in such functional learnings as critical reasoning, applications, and social behavior.

Some Recent Trends

Tools and machines are often developed in response to emerging needs. Hence, their development in itself represents educational change and their subsequent uses often contribute to further change. Several recent illustrations can be cited. The rise of nonparametric statistical methods has been notable since 1950, and particularly during the last eight or ten years. Electric test-scoring machines that can turn out more than 400 objective test scores per hour were introduced in the late 1930s. Electronic test-scoring machines that can process 6,000 answer sheets per hour first came into use in the middle 1950s. Electronic computers, or highly elaborate data processing machines, have been known for not much more than a decade. One illustration of the importance of such equipment is that Project Talent would have been an impossibility prior to the development of the high-speed electronic data processing and test-scoring equipment.

Some of the recent changes in education that can be classed as primarily administrative in nature are the ungraded school, the year-around school, flexible scheduling of classes, and team teaching, all of which apply to the elementary and secondary schools. It is possible to add at least the trimester plan and some of the newer methods of acceleration that are primarily operative at the college level. Educational television and language laboratories apply both to high schools and colleges. Although some attempts have been made to evaluate changes of these types, and doubtless other attempts are now under way, the majority of publications on these topics to date have either presented opinions or have consisted of descriptive and expository statements.[43] Hence, there is a real need for evaluative studies of these newly introduced programs in order to obtain evidence about their effectiveness.

There remain for brief discussion a number of changes that have recently been made in the instructional program of the schools.

[43]John F. Kourmadas and others, "Some Examples of Change," *Bulletin of the National Association of Secondary-School Principals,* 47:33–144; May, 1963; Jack Culbertson, Issue Editor, "Changing the Schools," *Theory into Practice,* 2:249–94, December, 1963.

They range from the introduction of programed learning and teaching machines to specialized changes in some school subjects, and they are not always based on either theoretical or empirical foundations. Some of the changes are so innovative that they are not likely to be evaluated beyond an exploratory level in their early stages. Consequently, the findings and conclusions arrived at to date must be considered tentative. But there are several instances in the school subjects where the resistance to change in the face of accepted theory and incontrovertible research evidence is striking.

Programed Instruction. Thorndike and Gates perhaps anticipated programed instruction in 1929 when they envisioned much instruction by the printed page if "a book could be so arranged that only to him who had done what was directed on page one would page two become visible, and so on."[44] Pressey invented a teaching machine several years earlier that involved instant "feedback" on success or failure of the learner and the necessity of his responding to a question correctly before moving to the next question.[45]

It remained for B. F. Skinner a quarter century later to revive the basic idea through provision of instant reinforcement of success, whether by the use of actual machines or by programed instruction by means of special books.[46] Controversies between exponents of several different methods of programing and overcommercialization by makers of some of the machines, as well as several more intrinsically important considerations, have resulted in a recent expression of belief by Pressey, who was probably the originator of the movement, that "current autoinstruction is *not* up to the claims made for it." Consequently, he called for a critical study not only to determine whether present methods are good "but also to determine whether an entirely different approach may not be better."[47]

Simplified Typewriter Keyboard. An event of significance for business education occurred in the middle 1930s when Dvorak devised a simplified keyboard for the typewriter based on research conducted according to Taylor's principles of time and motion study. The original alphabetically arranged Sholes keyboard, designed for

[44]Edward L. Thorndike and Arthur I. Gates, *Elementary Principles of Education,* New York: Macmillan, 1929, p. 242.

[45]Sidney L. Pressey, "A Simple Apparatus Which Gives Tests and Scores—and Teaches," *School and Society,* 23:373–76, March 20, 1926.

[46]"The Science of Learning and the Art of Teaching," *Harvard Education Review,* 24:86–97, Spring, 1954.

[47]Sidney L. Pressey, "Teaching Machine (and Learning Theory) Crisis," *Journal of Applied Psychology,* 47:1–6, February, 1963.

a hunt-and-peck, two-finger typing style, had been revised many times without sound reasons to support the changes that were made. The present standard keyboard overloads the left hand and the least agile fingers, underloads the "home row," and demands too many finger "jumps" from row to row.[48] One of Dvorak's students in an extensive series of studies found the simplified keyboard to be easier to learn, faster and more accurate to operate, and less fatiguing than the standard keyboard.[49] Despite a rather widespread acceptance of the simplified keyboard as superior to the traditional one, obstacles stand in the way of what seems to be progress: the cost of a changeover ($15 or so), coupled with the tripartite facts that (1) Business offices do not have them because their typists don't know how to use them; (2) Business schools don't use them in teaching because students do not demand training on them; and (3) Typewriter manufacturers don't provide them because of a lack of demand.[50] Almost no attention to the possibility of effecting this changeover occurs in the current literature of business education.

English. In composition and English, the battle between theorists and practitioners still rages. More than a half-century ago the disciplinary values of formal grammar were found to be unsupported by any scientific evidence, but textbooks have incorporated few fundamental changes in the traditional system of grammar they present, and teachers in most classrooms have perpetuated the teaching of formal grammar rather than the teaching of functional grammar through the media of written and oral composition.[51]

Mathematics and Science. A number of new programs have been developed for mathematics and science since the late 1950s. Some of them are the School Mathematics Study Group (SMSG) and the University of Illinois Arithmetic Project (UIAP), originated at the same institution; the Biological Science Curriculum Study (BSCS); the Chemical Education Material Study (CHEM); and the Physical Science Study Committee (PSSC) in physics. Their

[48]August Dvorak, "There Is a Better Typewriter Keyboard," *National Business Education Quarterly,* 12:51ff., December, 1943.

[49]Dwight D. W. Davis, "An Evaluation of the Simplified Typewriter Keyboard through an Analysis of Student Typewriting Errors on the Universal and Dvorak-Dealey Simplified Keyboard," *Journal of Business Education,* 10:10–11, May, 1935; 10:10ff., June, 1935; 11:21ff., September, 1935; 11:19–21, October, 1935.

[50]Jack Brown, "The Simplified Keyboard," *Journal of Business Education,* 27:326ff., April, 1952.

[51]John R. Searles and G. Robert Carlsen, "English," *Encyclopedia of Educational Research,* 3d ed., New York: Macmillan, 1960, pp. 454–70.

similarities include increased emphases on understandings and modern needs as substitutes for the traditional patterns which, in the case of mathematics, are very similar to those of 1890. In all instances, comparisons of the new program with its predecessor is difficult if not presently impossible because of a lack of common goals and consequently of valid measuring instruments.[52]

Modern Foreign Languages. The modern foreign languages have been strongly influenced by the intensive language programs in the armed services during World War II. The emphasis of those programs on the aural-oral, i.e., listening and speaking, skills has greatly influenced teaching in the high schools and may to some degree be responsible for the Foreign Language in the Elementary School (FLES) program. The aural-oral emphasis is largely responsible for introduction of language laboratories and educational TV as well as for the renewed emphasis on oral testing of language skills by the use of records and tapes.[53]

Reading and Listening. In the area of receptive language, there are three patterns of events worthy of mention. These are a controversy over the best method of teaching reading, a proposed change in the manner of introducing beginners to reading, and a change resulting from increased attention to listening as a skill.

The controversy over the best method of teaching reading arose when Flesch in *Why Johnny Can't Read,* published in 1955, contended that there was no evidence to support the "whole word," or "look-and-say," method, and that the phonic method is definitely superior.[54]

One reaction of the many that appeared over a period of years concluded that "Flesch misrepresented a number of research studies" and pointed out that his contrast of the two methods is misleading because his "old-style" method of teaching phonics is inferior to modern methods, including incidental use of phonics.[55] After an intensive study of the voluminous research findings on methods of teaching reading, Gray concluded pessimistically that

[52]Paul D. Hurd and Mary B. Rowe, "Science in the Secondary School," *Review of Educational Research,* 34:286–97, June, 1964; Donald J. Dessart, "Mathematics in the Secondary School," *Review of Educational Research,* 34:298–312, June, 1964.

[53]Emma M. Birkmaier, "Modern Languages," *Encyclopedia of Educational Research,* 3d ed., New York: Macmillan, 1960, pp. 861–88.

[54]Rudolf Flesch, *Why Johnny Can't Read, and What You Can Do About It,* New York: Harper and Brothers, 1955, p. 60.

[55]John B. Carroll, "The Case of Dr. Flesch," *American Psychologist,* 11:158–63, March, 1956.

"the results of research do not indicate conclusively which of the various methods now in use is the best."[56]

A second noteworthy recent event in reading is the invention of the Initial Teaching Alphabet (i/t/a) by Pitman, grandson of the founder of the Pitman Shorthand System. The i/t/a uses 44 symbols—24 are standard English letters and 20 are special symbols designed to supplement the more familiar ones. In contrast with English, in which a sound may be spelled in several ways and a combination of letters may be pronounced in more than one way, i/t/a provides a one-to-one relationship between symbol and sound, and hence is phonemic rather than phonetic. Moreover, capital letters are merely enlargements of lower-case letters.[57] Results of research show that children learn faster and more effectively with this system than with standard English and make effective transfer to the usual English alphabet very soon after learning to read by i/t/a.[58] One of the American educators who has experimented extensively with the system concluded that it is "the most serviceable pattern that has up to now been proven workable in introducing the child to the reading and writing process."[59]

Listening, sometimes called "auding," first received the direct attention of researchers in the middle 1950s. Its importance as a receptive language skill is evidenced by the recent development of standardized tests for listening, by direct attention to the teaching of listening in many present-day classrooms, and by a list of 743 references on this topic compiled in 1961.[60]

Social Studies. An event that produced violent reactions but far less obvious educational change was the publication of an article in the April 4, 1943, issue of the *New York Times* that attacked the teaching of American history in high schools as grossly inadequate.[61] The attack was based on results and conclusions of a study in which two historians administered a highly unreliable "questionnaire" consisting entirely of recall questions dealing with detailed and often inconsequential facts of American history to some 7000 college

[56]William S. Gray, "The Teaching of Reading," *Encyclopedia of Educational Research,* 3d ed., New York: Macmillan, 1960, p. 1122.

[57]*The Story of i/t/a,* New York: Initial Teaching Alphabet Publications, Inc., 1965.

[58]William D. Boutwell, "An Easier Way to Learn to Read—i/t/a," *PTA Magazine,* 59:11–13, September, 1964.

[59]Albert J. Mazurkiewicz, "The Initial Teaching Alphabet for Reading? Yes!" *Educational Leadership,* 22:390ff., March, 1965.

[60]Sam Duker, "Listening," *Review of Educational Research,* 34:156–63, April, 1964.

[61]Benjamin Fine, "Ignorance of U. S. History Shown by College Freshmen," *New York Times,* April 4, 1943.

freshmen. Editorial comments and articles in the press and in educational journals dealt at length with the *pro* and *con* of the controversy that soon arose. The most constructive response was doubtless the publication of a book by representatives of several organizations of social scientists in which the conclusions reported in the *New York Times* article were, by inference, related as deplorable because of their dependence on unrealistic value judgments and in which it was contended that any reasonable standard in American history must be based on the records of what selected groups actually achieve rather than on "what a group of enthusiasts think should be the standard."[62] Despite the recommendations of this report that a total of thirty-four specific dates and ninety-five persons constitute the specific core of factual knowledge of these types, it was recently pointed out that "the bulk of American high schools have programs largely reflecting the suggestions made approximately forty years before."[63]

Since some commonly desired outcomes of the social studies cannot be measured while pupils are in school, and cannot in fact be evidenced in behavior until some years later, many studies of adult social behavior have direct implications for education, especially at the high-school level. The only such study that will be mentioned here dealt with the voting behavior of adults in national elections.[64] Three related trends are represented here by a few key facts from an extensive table: (1) The percentage of children aged five to seventeen enrolled in school increased from 65 in 1880 to 78 in 1920 and to 81 in 1948; (2) The percentage of secondary-school-age children enrolled in school increased from 7 in 1880 to 32 in 1920 and to 74 in 1948; and (3) The percentage of the electorate voting in presidential election years decreased from 87 in 1880 to a low of 48 in 1920, came back to a recent high of 63 in 1940, and decreased to a near low of 51 in 1948. The author concluded that to the extent the high school is responsible for developing in its pupils a disposition and ability to vote, the data indicate "a dismal failure of the educational institution."

FOUNDATIONS FOR EDUCATIONAL CHANGE

Finally, it is apparent that educational changes differ in the

[62]Edgar B. Wesley, Director, *American History in Schools and Colleges,* New York: Macmillan, 1944, p. 3.

[63]Richard E. Gross and Wm. V. Badger, "Social Studies," *Encyclopedia of Educational Research,* 3d ed., New York: Macmillan, 1960, p. 1298.

[64]Kermit A. Cook, "Voting Responsibility and the Public Schools," *Social Education,* 15:279–81, October, 1951.

degree to which they have lagged behind or forged ahead of theoretical formulations and educational research findings. On the one hand, Thorpe and Schmuller voiced the opinion that, "Methodology . . . has been the Princess of American education and theory its Cinderella."[65] However, the Greek goddess, Athena, is reported in mythology to have sprung full-blown from the forehead of her father, Zeus. In summary, both allusions seem applicable—the first to the slowness of some educational changes, and the second to the suddenness of others.

[65]Louis P. Thorpe and Allen M. Schmuller, *Contemporary Theories of Learning*, New York: Ronald Press, 1954, p. 10.

JOHN H. CHILCOTT

ANTHROPOLOGY AND THE STUDY OF EDUCATION

SINCE WORLD WAR II THERE HAS BEEN A FLORESCENCE OF INTEREST in anthropology. Bookstores and even supermarkets now offer a number of classical anthropological studies. There even has been a popular novel written about a noted anthropologist.[1] Undergraduate enrollment in anthropology courses has been one of the fastest growing areas of the liberal arts curriculum. It is not surprising, therefore, to discover that many prospective teachers as well as most scholars have either read something about anthropology or in a more formal fashion have included anthropological coursework in their program of study.

Anthropologists, like other scholars during the past decade, have become increasingly concerned with the nature of formal education in America. The mutual interest of teacher and anthropologist has provided an expanding body of theory and data related to the social processes of enculturation and education. The linkage of anthropology and education may also be due in part to the need for interdisciplinary research during an era of increasing specialization, and to the recent tendency of science to begin to focus on man himself.[2]

It is not the purpose of this paper to summarize the advances and the content of previous work in the area of anthropology and education. Several excellent summaries have already accomplished

[1] Irving Wallace, *Three Sirens,* New York: The New American Library, 1963.
[2] W. R. Shunk and B. Z. Goldstein, "Anthropology and Education," *Review of Educational Research,* Vol. 34, No. 1 (February, 1964), p. 71.

this, as have several textbooks, two of which incidentally were written by professors of education.[3] Rather, this paper will concentrate on providing a few examples of how anthropology may contribute to the future study of education.

At the outset it is perhaps important to attempt a distinction between anthropology and education. Anthropology is a scholarly discipline which concentrates on the study of man and his works. As such it has a subject matter, a theoretical framework, and a methodology to approach the subject matter. Education, on the other hand, is a social process. Those engaged in the institutionalized form of this social process are usually referred to as educators. In addition, there is a group of individuals who are involved in the training of educators, whose special sphere of research focuses on the educational process, and who classify themselves as professional educators. These professional educators utilize those facets of the scholarly disciplines, such as philosophy, psychology, and anthropology, which focus on the educational process. Thus, educators and professional educators alike need to be aware of those aspects of anthropology which may contribute to a better understanding of the educational process.

One of the major contributions of anthropology to social science theory has been the use of the concept of culture to explain human behavior. Of particular interest to the study of education are three characteristics of culture: namely, that culture is learned, that culture is shared, and that culture is patterned. The process of learning one's culture is referred to as enculturation. The anthropologist has developed a typology in which he distinguishes between enculturation, socialization, and education. Enculturation is the total process of learning one's culture and as such includes the other processes. Through *enculturation* the child learns by participating in the culture to develop a taste for a particular food or a preference for a particular smell. In this manner even covert culture is transmitted from one generation to another. *Socialization* is that phase of the enculturative process which is primarily concerned with learning social behavior in a culturally sanctioned direction. *Education* is that phase of the enculturative process which has been institutionalized and given direction. Thus, the successful educator must be concerned with the total process of enculturation. In order to alter or add to one segment of the cultural pattern, adjustments must be made to the remaining segments of the con-

[3]T. Brameld, *Cultural Foundations of Education,* New York: Harper and Row, 1957.

figuration. For example, if a teacher wishes to encourage the development of autonomous individuals among her students she needs to know that the cultural orientation, family structure, and role expectations are likewise encouraging autonomous behavior on the part of her students; if such is not the case, she may be encouraging frustration and social conflict. All too often our formal education is a cross-cultural transaction in the sense that the teacher represents one culture and the students another.

The fact that culture is shared is also of interest since the culture is never shared equally among all members of the society. There is differential sharing between the old and the young, between the sexes, between the chief and the commoner, and between the teacher and the students. Thus, the extent to which a teacher shares the general cultural heritage may limit or extend the culture which is being transmitted to the student.

The many problems associated with the transmission of culture have been treated at length by a number of distinguished anthropologists. There is one aspect of the nature of cultural transmission particularly important: that of transmitting the meaning of culture. "Communication is more than meaning, for it is meaning that is communicated."[4] Language provides a vehicle for the transmission of cultural ideas. Its verbal symbols enable man to transcend the immediate and the real, providing also an introduction to memories, hopes, and the fantasies peculiar to a given culture.[5] "As we learn our language, we acquire the cultural ideas with which it is freighted, without conscious realization that we are doing so. For example, God obviously is not endowed by Christianity with sexual qualities. He is always he; his son is born of woman, and God is referred to as the father. The images of a patriarchal society thus color our religious attitude through the very language which conveys them."[6]

Thus, if a child does not understand the meaning of the oral symbols or if he attributes a different meaning to the oral symbols than that attributed by the teacher, he may never acquire the social convention, the technical skill, or the perceptual framework which the teacher is intending to transmit. Of particular importance along these lines is the current work of Kimball at Columbia University.[7] Kimball's significant suggestions include:

[4]R. Ross, *Symbols and Civilization,* New York: Harcourt, Brace and World, Inc., 1963, p. 155.

[5]J. Bram, *Language and Society,* New York: Random House, 1955, p. 23.

[6]R. Ross, *op. cit.,* p. 157.

[7]S. Kimball, "The Transmission of Culture," *Educational Horizons,* VR XVIII, p. 161–86.

The process of education is more than formal techniques which indicate a historical bias toward the individual. The individual is innately good, innately bad, and so on. We must also study the environment which includes cultural behavior and which can be divided into the conditioning on one hand, and the arrangement of experiences into new combinations which we label cognition on the other. Thus, we have teaching which emphasizes rote learning, the teaching of skills, and we also have teaching which helps the student utilize experience to frame questions, the answers to which express relationships. The latter approach avoids assigning fixed attributes to an individual. Education therefore must focus on the influences which shape the child. To date little effort has been made to describe the cognitive environment of the child-training operation. We must do this in order to develop an adequate model of learning. It has already been noted how the culture, and especially the language of culture, tends to reflect the cognitive style of the particular culture so that the cultural experience of the child is filtered through a cultural perspective and is interpreted to the child's world view of the culture. For example, in America time is measured on a horizontal basis; that is, time moves from the past to the present to the future. There is a movement and most children become future-time-oriented. The way they view school, the way they view play, and the way they ultimately view work will be on the basis of the future. On the other hand, we have the Latin-American concept of time which is vertical; time is not in movement —rather the past is part of today and so is the future. Since time is stationary, there is little future-time orientation. Thus, a Latin-American child learns to perceive work and play in terms of the present. It is today that is important, and not tomorrow. Since the cultural patterning affects the nature of learning, the Latin-American child who comes to this country has a difficult time accepting the reward-sanction system of American schools wherein the rewards are delayed for considerable periods of time. The American child has been conditioned to deny rewards until the future whereas the Latin child seeks immediate rewards.

The process of education therefore includes the acquisition of the tools with which the world can be apprehended symbolically. The patterns of differentiation of things, events, relationships, and processes, these constitute the basic intellectual efforts in learning; these are the subject matter of education. The acquisition of these tools can be accomplished in some cultures through mythology and sacred ceremonies or, as in the case of American culture, these tools may be organized into formal courses. Thus, Kimball suggests that every culture possesses categories of knowledge, that every culture can classify individuals, qualities, events, processes. He also indicates the need of every culture to discriminate, to categorize, and he observes that all cultures develop the criteria on which these categories are based and the laws which govern their selection. Thus, among some American Indian cultures, objects, persons, and behaviors are classified as to whether they are dangerous or safe, friendly or hostile.

In addition to categories of knowledge and laws which govern their selection, there are also cultural processes. How do things happen? What is the relationship between emergence, becoming, being, and ending? Kimball suggests that these concepts are the tools of cognition. Thus, since early childhood sets the stage for what comes later, knowledge of the preparation of the infant for responding to cultural experiences should be a basic concern of education. To date, conceptual conditions which affect the transmission of culture have been left largely implicit in educational theory. The rules which govern the organization and evaluation of knowledge and explain change are found here.

There is an additional dimension to Kimball's anthropological model of learning which would make a significant contribution to the learning process. Most of us have had the experience of trying to learn something with a slightly different cognitive style than that with which we are already familiar—the "new math," or a foreign language, for example. What may make this process difficult is the rigidity with which the cultural categories are inculcated in older members of a society. Thus it may be easier to teach young children a variant cognitive style and permit them more flexibility with respect to their categorizing of the cultural elements. Not only is the nature of the categorizing process important, but the developmental process of categorizing is equally important.

Out of the methodology of anthropology emerges an approach which may prove to be exceptionally useful for the study of education. The cross-cultural approach to education—that is, inquiry into the operation of the same or similar educational process in various cultures—permits the educator to view education in America more objectively. When we compare the disciplinary agents of a non-literate society such as an American Indian group with those of middle-class Anglo Americans, some interesting insights emerge. In the non-literate society, the agents are usually outside the immediate circle of relatives—his mother's brother for a boy, for example—or these agents may consist of cannibalistic spirits who run off the recalcitrants.[8] The immediate relatives usually maintain a loving, protecting relationship with the child. In the Anglo society, however, the parent is on the one hand a protector and on the other hand a disciplinarian. Disciplinarians outside the home are strangers—the policeman, or teacher, who may not be counted on to show mercy. Recalcitrants are punished by denying foodstuffs, trips, movies, objects, and events which bring pleasures to the child. Thus, in the non-literate society some security is always available, whereas security may be extremely difficult to find either in terms of persons or objects in the Anglo society.

Still other insights which have emerged from cross-cultural comparisons are:

1. That the status of the teacher appears to be lowered as a society shifts from a sacred to a secular culture.

2. That as a society becomes urbanized the adult roles are further removed from the experience of the child. (A child has no idea what his father does in a factory or office; all he knows is that he comes home "crabby.")

3. That modern societies lack traditions through which the child may be socialized, and consequently the group serves as a major sanctioning agency.

4. That cultural limits on the behavior of different age groups (the teen-ager) tend to become more restrictive in modern societies.

5. That the use of the supernatural as a disciplinary mechanism wanes as the child becomes more aware, through science, of the forces which direct his world.

The cross-cultural approach could develop considerable sophistication in describing American education through the use of Jules Henry's *Cross-Cultural Outline of Education*; however, to date little use has been made of this instrument.[9] One of Henry's provocative observations of education in modern societies is that the amount of information available to teach has increased tremendously, whereas the number of techniques to teach the additional information has remained relatively the same.

Of particular importance to the study of education would be a series of basic ethnographic studies of the school culture utilizing the field methods of anthropology. The resulting data would include descriptions of the housing, material culture, social patterns of

[8]G. Pettitt, *Primitive Education in North America,* Chapter IV.
[9]J. Henry, "A Cross-Cultural Outline of Education," *Current Anthropology,* Vol. 1, No. 4 (July, 1960), pp. 267–93.

speech, age-grading practices, an interactional analysis both internal and external, social structure, social roles, value orientations, attitudes, folklore, the process of culture change and innovation, and the cognitive style of the school. Once these data were gathered, we could then examine the possibility of the existence of educational "cultural areas" which have been created through the influence of "local control." Or the data might reveal that in reality "school cultures" everywhere are so similar that we possess, in spite of the ideals of local control of education, a national school system.

Such ethnographic data might also demonstrate any discontinuity which may exist between the school culture and the student culture, or between the school culture and the community culture. Should these discontinuities become too severe, the student may lose interest and drop out. There needs to be a "cultural fit" between the culture represented by the school and the culture of the student, otherwise school remains meaningless for him. As McKeel has suggested, the educational system may not work for a child who has been trained in a different cultural setting by different methods and standards.[10] Some of the Bureau of Indian Affairs schools provide a graphic example of lack of cultural fit between the school culture and the cultures of the students. Finally, such data might also suggest any discontinuity which may exist between the cognitive style of the school and the ideal of "American Education" as perceived at the national level.

Of particular interest to many anthropologists and of considerable significance to the future of American education would be an analysis of the process of culture change both at the level of the school and in American education. Such an analysis would include the isolation of the factors which inhibit or encourage school culture change, the nature and role of educational innovators, the dissemination of innovations, and finally the degree of cultural lag between educational institutions and changes in the American culture. At the national level it would be profitable to examine the nature and direction of cultural drift in education. Such an analysis would provide clues as to just how far a school may go in serving as an agent of change and just how much the culture does in the *final* analysis determine the course of human events.

So far, nothing has been mentioned of culture and personality. This is an extensive topic and it has been adequately covered in the literature. Perhaps we might determine the existence of a modal

---

[10]S. Mekeel, "Education, Child Training and Culture," *American Journal of Sociology*, Vol. 48, 1943, pp. 676–81.

successful teaching personality. Most of us have had the experience of a student who though unsuccessful in our courses has become an outstanding teacher, or the student who did well in the college class but who wouldn't face the students during student teaching. If such personalities exist, it may be an easier process to select prospective teachers on the basis of a personality profile than on their progress in the College of Education. At the same time it would also be interesting to discover the limits which the school culture may place on personality types, beyond which the teacher would be unsuccessful.

It is apparent that a serious need exists to both describe in depth and to give a quantitative basis to many of our generalizations about education.[11] The usual survey type of research common to so much of education will not provide an adequate basis from which educational predictions can be made. Just as the anthropologist cannot adequately describe a culture on the basis of a two-week visit, neither can the study of education be successful unless detailed, lengthy studies of the nature of education are conducted.

This is only a sample of the contributions which anthropology might make to the study of education. Nothing has been mentioned concerning the contributions which linguistics could make to language teaching, or those which physical anthropology could make to child growth and development. In the applied area, anthropology might contribute to developing better educational programs for the children of ethnic minorities. Anthropology could also frame the school curriculum so as to reduce international misunderstanding. Anthropology must contribute to the development of educational programs and teacher-training programs for teaching in a foreign country where the *culture* is so drastically different from the American culture, where the cultural perception of education may vary drastically from the American, where the reward-sanction system utilized in the American school may not exist, or where the needs of the society may be much simpler than those facing an industrialized society. In short, I am suggesting that we cannot export American education *per se.* What is needed in the "undeveloped" countries is a program of education which is created on the spot and designed on the basis of problem solving to meet the requirements of the local population. An anthropologically trained educator would be aware of the cultural factors affecting education as well as the nature of the felt needs of the local population, and on the

[11] C. Kluckhohn, "Theoretical Basis for an Empirical Method of Studying The Acquisition of Culture by an Individual," *Man,* Vol. 39 (1939), pp. 98–103.

basis of such knowledge would create an educational program which would account for the cultural barriers to education.

In this all too brief survey, there has been an attempt to provide an anthropological point of view and approach which the educator might find useful in creating an understanding of both the process of education and the cultural environment which affects student behavior. If, as Franz Boas said in 1928, "the task of the future is to free ourselves from the shades of traditional thinking while preserving what is good and useful from the past,"[12] then anthropological theory and methodology can be most useful to the study of education. For anthropology presently fulfills in relation to the behavioral sciences the role formerly filled by philosophy in relation to all sciences.[13] Many anthropologists and educators agree with Theodore Brameld who suggests that the separation of anthropology and education is in itself a cultural product brought about by specialization and complacency.[14]

It seems that man *can* control his own life and that the scientific method is the chief instrument to enable him to do so. Thus, the use of the science of anthropology in the study of educational processes will, through increased cross fertilization, aid man in understanding the complexity of society today and in the future.

[12]F. Boas, *Anthropology and Modern Life,* New York: W. W. Norton, 1962.

[13]V. Ray, "Objectives for a Liberal Education," *The Teaching of Anthropology,* 1963, pp. 589–94.

[14]T. Brameld, *Education for the Emerging Age,* New York: Harper and Row, 1961.

T. Frank Saunders

ORIGINALITY IN AMERICAN PHILOSOPHY: EDUCATIONAL PERSPECTIVES

Before 1860, America was an unlikely ground for fertile philosophic thought. Although eighteenth-century colonials were acquainted with Locke and Newton, they were steeped in the "genteel tradition" which paid little attention to philosophy and gave less prestige to scientific inquiry. The prevailing mood was to dream for a life of rural elegance and dignity, the world for which Twain, Bellamy, and Adams hoped. This mood stifled the growth of science in America until the middle of the nineteenth century.

Harvard, as an example of the times, was a college well stocked with scientific instruments and yet teachers were content to duplicate experiments originated in other parts of the world. As a Puritan college, Harvard was content to know about science without engaging in it. In effect, Harvard was an institution interested in science absorption but without interest in scientific inquiry.

About the time of Charles Darwin's evolutionary theory, certain converging events were preparing groundwork for the emergence of scientific philosophy as a new social force and as a personal justification for the lives of some of the thinkers of the era.

Darwin's writings were more than a sign of the times—they were a prophecy that quantification and empiricism were soon to be rules by which man would think and conduct investigations.

Add the evolutionary insult to man's divine origins, accompanied by the industrial revolution, urbanization, and the mobility now possible with the railroads, and the "genteel tradition" of Americans became a dream found only in romantic literature.

81

Social consciousness was aroused by family fragmentation, dislocation of individuals, and uprooted traditional ethics and religious standards. Soon spokesmen were in search of a viable new framework in which Americans could regain their identity. The climate for modern science was at hand.

The "golden era" of American philosophy was ushered in by the works of Peirce, Royce, Santayana, Dewey, James, Lewis, and others. These writers dominated the American philosophic scene at the turn of the century. Their contributions to the new spirit developing in America helped bring to fruition many significant findings of science.

C. S. Peirce and John Dewey might be viewed as candidates for the title of "original thinkers." Pragmatic philosophy can be seen as the vehicle of their greatness, and pragmatism has been a distinctive contribution of American philosophic thought to philosophy in general. From the flyleaf of Gallie's book on Peirce we read:

Some people, indeed, would now claim that the width and depth of his scientific culture and his astonishing combination of critical perseverence with constructive power entitled Peirce to rank as the most original philosopher of the 19th Century.[1]

While it would be interesting to explore the choleric personality characteristics of C. S. Peirce, we are more concerned with his philosophy than with the man himself. Noting that Peirce was of the nineteenth century (1839–1919) provides some insight into the astonishing depth of philosophic thought which he developed. His contributions to American philosophy have long been neglected although he is attaining some measure of recognition at the present time.

What is the source of Peirce's pragmatic doctrine? The history of philosophy testifies to the notion that no concept is fully determined by the originator of that concept. Philosophic concepts are especially difficult to trace since they are generally problems or questions rather than solutions or answers. Adding to the claim that knowledge is always a process in which fuller meaning is developed, Peirce writes, "any philosophical doctrine that should be completely new could hardly fail to prove completely false."

What exactly is the idea which has had such an impact on philosophy and science? In essence, pragmatism is a criterion of meaning. The criterion is used to assert that the meaning of a con-

[1]See W. B. Gallie, *Peirce and Pragmatism,* London: Penguin, 1952.

cept is to be found in its usage or consequences. More specifically, Peirce writes, ". . . If one can define accurately all the conceivable experimental phenomena which the affirmation or denial of a concept could imply, one will have therein a complete definition of the concept, and *there is absolutely nothing in it.*"[2]

Peirce noted two major features of pragmatism. First, it specifies the conditions under which language is meaningful; second, it locates the meanings of propositions in the determinate consequences of those propositions. What is the impact on inquiry or teaching of these conceptions? We teach children that terms or symbols have referents.

The symbol "apple" refers to O. Moreover, the interpretant "fruit" helps locate the object and gives distinct meaning to the symbol, as "apple"

Fruit⟍⟋O

However, if we are to change the category or interpretant of fruit to modern physics the symbol would now refer to a whirling molecular mass or set of meter readings as

"apple"

Modern physics

The symbol then refers to the object, determined by the system of interpreting ideas. The rather unusual character of pragmatism is the junction that *all three* components—symbol, interpretant, and referent—*must* be present for *any* meaning at all to emerge.

Further, any consequences determined by this process of establishing meaning must be sharable and public in nature. The consequences must have been so derived as to permit duplication by any investigator trained to such inquiry. Intuition, personal reference, and private meaning are rejected as nonsensical and indeterminate.

These demands on language meaning were to have far-reaching and extensive consequences for American thinkers as well as to philosophers on the continent. Indeed, American philosophy can be judged to be a footnote to Peirce.

Every thinker puts some portion of an apparently stable world in peril and no one can wholly predict what will emerge in its place.[3]

[2]Justus Buchler, *Philosophical Writings of Peirce,* New York: Dover Publications, Inc., 1955, p. 252.

[3]Joseph Ratner, *Intelligence in the Modern World,* New York: The Modern Library, 1939, Frontispiece.

William James, in his enthusiasm to popularize Peirce's pragmatism and explicate his own version of the many ramifications of the theory, became intrigued by the practical character of pragmatism and insisted *it was not just a meaning* theory but a truth criterion.[4] Loosely his formulation went, "If it works, it is true." Further, he claimed the right of each individual to judge when it was true and *for what* it worked. Thus, if it pleased or satisfied the individual (worked for him), the idea was true. This "confused semiotic" carried with it the religious and ambiguous characteristics of all psychologism and subjectively verifiable questions.[5]

James saw pragmatism as a kind of practicalism more akin to etiological derivation of the Greek term pragma.[6] His practicalism, as a theory of truth which rejected the necessity of any publicly sharable, openly verifiable reference, brought James' peers down about his head.

Peirce was forced to rename his theory to distinguish it from the one James was popularizing. The new name he used was pragmaticism, which he held was "ugly enough to be safe from pirates."[7]

Russell and Holmes attacked James' practicalism on the base that convenience or satisfaction are inadequate criteria by which to verify investigation or value.[8] Peirce wanted to avoid James' truth notion and his "personal satisfaction theory." *He did not want pragmatism wedded to action.*

Few modern philosophers favor James as a pragmatist, and his rejection continues. Frederic Neff, in a crystal-clear description of pragmatism, sees Peirce as brilliant, James as witty, and Dewey as profound.[9]

James' and Peirce's pragmatism have been syncretistically fused in the mind of the public. There is the continued claim that these forms are matters of individual preference. However, there is greater logical than psychological polarity between them. Truth for the one is found in symbolic logic, while Jacob's ladder suffices for the other. "Growth itself is the only moral end."[10]

John Dewey is remembered for his reformulation of pragmatism as instrumentalism and his greatest impact has been on the educational scene rather than in the philosophic arena.

[4]Morton White, *The Age of Analysis,* New York: Mentor Books, 1955, p. 160.

[5]Arthur Bentley, *Knowing and the Known,* Boston: Beacon Press, 1949, Ch. IX.

[6]William James, *Pragmatism,* New York, 1907, p. 46.

[7]Buchler, *op. cit.,* p. 255.

[8]Bertrand Russell, *Philosophical Essays,* London, 1910, Chapter 5.

[9]Frederic Neff, "Pragmatism and Education," *Philosophy of Education,* ed. by H. W. Burns and C. J. Brauner, New York: Ronald Press, 1962, p. 304.

[10]John Dewey, *Reconstruction in Philosophy,* Boston, 1948, p. 164.

Instrumentalism, for Dewey, "is an attempt to constitute a precise logical theory of concepts, of judgments and inferences in their various forms, by considering primarily how thought functions in the experimental determination of future consequences."[11]

Dewey's extension of the "consequences" of Peirce's pragmatism to moral instrumentalities in the open community imported new questions which had considerable significance to the education profession.

Dewey's thinking was original to American philosophy. In many ways his most important ideas were (1) a focus on thought as a means-ends method continuum; (2) the growth principle; and (3) the extension of intelligence to art constructions.

A consideration of the means-ends method continuum reveals that it represents a reversal of traditional learning theory. The goals and processes of education must be reframed.

In the first instance any means is *helpless without a goal clearly formulated*, for any goal precisely (pragmatically) constructed becomes an agent of its own attainment. The goal of a "chocolate cake" rejects means found in a lumber yard and selects its means from a range of culinary components.

The recipe offers replication once the pattern of inquiry is set, thereby emphasizing the importance of *method* in the process of inquiry. To separate means from ends, then, is to artificate both. To neglect method is to reduce inquiry to caprice.

Dewey's growth principle is more in the nature of a moral rule. This principle suggests that the goal of man is the extension and refinement of human qualities in ever unfolding futures. "Growth for the sake of growth" is a principle designed to insure the autonomy of inquiry. It is a formulation proposing that criteria of merit must select alternatives which themselves promote wider ranges of alternatives. Thus means-ends methods expansions are most moral. They are most likely to promote open inquiry. *To block inquiry is the paradigm of immorality.*

Probably the most powerful idea Dewey developed was his concept of quality. This concept may yet bring about a revolution in philosophic aesthetics and thereby in educational theory.

Dewey's *Art as Experience*[12] was a major innovation not only in the consideration of art as basic to intelligence but also in locating science as the handmaiden to the arts. Artistic construction

---

[11]"The Development of American Pragmatism" in *Studies in the History of Ideas,* Vol. 11, New York, 1925, p. 367.

[12]See John Dewey, *Art as Experience,* New York: Capricorn Books, 1958.

was dignified as an intelligent operation and not the usual release of "emotional pressures" (Hirn) and "neurotic avoidance" (Freud).

Art must not become the beauty parlor of the civilization, says Dewey, but should find its way into the very essence of human meaning.

Construction that is artistic is as much a case of genuine thought as that expressed in scientific and philosophical matters, and so in all genuine aesthetic appreciation of art, since the latter must in some way, to be vital, retrace the course of the creative process.[13]

Can we assume that Dewey is using the word "construction" in a sense not generally accorded the term? He certainly is asserting that science is properly in service to art. Yet once we remove the helpmate of "intelligence" or control from the "irrational," "emotional" art process can we continue to refer to art as constructed or ordered? Can we talk about education as moral and aesthetic without the "constructions" of science?

While Dewey outlined the necessity for the priority of art experience, he left to others the responsibility to design a method by which the entire conception of intelligence might be expanded to make room for the aesthetic process as a respectable endeavor issuing its own discourse, language, categories, and curricular proposals.

Current investigations are striving desperately to "save" aesthetics for society and school. Currently the demand is for a system, which must entail language, categories, and inquiry, i.e., an expanded conception of intelligence, which will elevate art activity to its place in world affairs. Some see art not only as a peer of science but as the very point of science.

Probably the most significant development since Dewey's introduction of "art experience" into life and education is to be found in a movement started by Francis Villemain and Nathaniel Champlin toward a concept of qualitative controls.[14]

Using Dewey's conception of "art experience" and Peirce's conception of symbols, this new movement redefines intelligence to mean a process or ongoing activity of relating symbols where there might be most significant meanings in a qualitative aesthetic sense.

The concept of "qualitative problem solving" emerges to rehabilitate the "nonrational" activities of artists. This concept prom-

---

[13]John Dewey, *Philosophy and Civilization,* New York: Minton Balch and Co., 1931, p. 116.

[14]"Frontiers for an Experimental Philosophy of Education," *The Antioch Review,* XIX, 1959, pp. 345–59.

ises a future with a new range of possible inquiries and directions for education, with new categories of curricula which emerge from a long history wherein educational meaning requires clear specification in a "shared society." The use of categories and concepts on aesthetic fronts is educational activity at its best. As Champlin says:

> For, if the hypothesis herein advanced is tested and found to hold, then we must be willing to give up the emotional theory, the notion that art experience is restricted either to the "fine arts" or to the departments of art education, the view that theory is of value only when it leads immediately to non-theory (practice) and the conception that removes from the domain of public education those qualitative moments of sympathy, sorrow, "celebration of ideals realized" so precious to shared living and so important to sustain us during turning points in our personal lives. It remains to be seen whether or not we will pay the price.[15]

The "qualitative moments" as instances of *intelligent action* force the conception of intelligence to be reevaluated. It is no longer a category of psychology. As qualitative problem solving gains structure (Dewey's "construction"), education may incorporate the enriched "intelligent" qualities.

Education can then be seen as the development of categories for symbolizing (problem solving), the reconstruction of these categories as they are extended to include aesthetic concerns, and a reflexive "double think" about the very process of both the "development" and the "reconstruction" (using the "process of judgment" as the subject matter of some more inclusive generic judgment).

How does the notion of quality enter the moral sphere? Can the question of "oughts" and "shoulds" ever be placed in a present or past context? Does education for instrumentalism become a matter for the indicative or the imperative moods?

Education across the world has one common meaning. Education everywhere is designed to implant, preserve, and foster the values held by the community at large. That the educative process entails skill training distinguishes vocational education from education in the wider sense. *The pragmatic addition draws attention to the imperative character of value judgment.* To say for instance "Don't kill that man," after the man has been killed, is a meaningless injunction. "You should not kill" is always a future or imperative claim.

If education is value laden, and values are imperative rather than indicative in character, then education is clearly a matter not only of *future value formulations* but of developing criteria for

---

[15]Nathaniel Champlin, "John Dewey: Beyond the Centennial," *Educational Leadership,* 1960.

the selection between these alternate and often incompatible formulations.

The polemic emerging is a rejection of cultural transmission and value preservation in favor of cultural reconstruction and training in value inquiry.

Thus, pragmatism insists that one can never be original if there is an absence of training or competence. Pragmatism suggests that "original" designates a value claim and not a clear descriptive referent.

Originality by this rule then becomes not only a value term but an assertion of expertness in the area to be investigated. Originality emerges from more than ignorance: it is minimal competence —it is significant error at least. The accolade "original" found in other types of situations may be used or abused due to an absence of criteria by which to evaluate the product involved. The chimpanzee's painting is hardly original when the "deliberately constructed" criterion is employed. Indeed, the animal's products are forever insulated from the location of competence framed in terms of *competing alternatives*. One has difficulty conceiving the chimp's *decision* to do cubism rather than random splashings.

Originality in thought then is possible only with the imperative, and not indicative, constructions in areas of competence beyond competence.

In summary, it is suggested that aesthetic judgments gain their adequacy in part by remaining "outside the human skin" both for objects of attention and sources of judgment, while education can gain its meaning only as it appeals to the category of aesthetic-value constructions where the conception of the qualitative permits a purchase on value and quality as methodizing procedures.

Floyd A. Miller

STATE GOVERNMENT AND PUBLIC EDUCATION

In this year of 1966, we are surrounded with social and economic changes which defy description. There are great changes, some of them awesome—and some frequently devastating in their destruction of status quos.

Just as relentlessly as change tries the mettle of men and women, changes try the courage, the integrity, and the usefulness of governments. In this country, some leaders believe that state governments are affected most of all. Because of its position in the hierarchy of governments, the state feels the wild winds of change beating on it from both sides. Because it stands squarely between the federal government and the local, it inherits problems of both. This is true of every arm of the state government, because education is so pre-eminently the business of state governments, and because education is so involved in all change. State departments of education are confronted with the complexities of society at large.

The state department of education has responsibilities not unlike those of the second or third runner on a relay team. It is pressed from one direction by citizens and communities to come to their aid on the problems of local schools. In addition, it looks to the federal government for assistance in the development of new programs needed in every state and locality. And if it drops the baton, history alone will tell us how costly the fumble.

The unique position of states and state departments of education may very well be better understood at the federal level than elsewhere. In Detroit in 1964, Commissioner Keppel of the U. S.

89

Office of Education described this position very simply and succinctly when he said:

But the strategic link between America's 30,000 autonomous school districts and Washington is within our States—and it is here that American
education today will ultimately meet or fail to meet the extraordinary
challenges of our time.

Speaking at a joint Conference of State Board members,
Commissioners of Education and Legislators in Portland, Oregon,
in early 1966, Wayne O. Reed, a top official in the U. S. Office of
Education, said: "Now for the first time the Congress is saying to
the state departments of education in tones both loud and clear:
'Be strong! Gird yourselves for change and challenge. And here is
money to help you.'" This statement implies a recognition of the
importance of state departments of education, as well as of their
weaknesses. It trumpets a call to arms.

The history of American public education tells us that state
departments of education developed or "growed up" in a "Topsy-
like" fashion, somewhat simultaneously with the development of
important American principles such as: public education is free;
public education is universal; public education is non-sectarian;
and public education is compulsory. The steps in this evolution
range from a department of education such as was established by
Horace Mann in 1837 when at the age of forty-two he sold his law
books and became secretary to the first state board of education
in Massachusetts at a salary of $1500, to the present sophisticated
and extremely effective State Department of Education in New
York.

Public education is primarily a state function under the federal
and state constitutions. Of necessity, state departments of education were developed. Except for the right of the federal government
to engage in educational activities under its constitutionally delegated and implied powers, and subject only to general constitutional limitations, authority for public education is vested in the state
governments. The state may or may not delegate its power to
organize and operate schools to its own political subdivisions, such
as school districts. If it has delegated such power, the state may at
any time reverse its policy, reclaim this power, and operate the
public schools itself. States also have varying amounts of authority
over all other institutions of education, both public and private.

In terms of structure, state departments of education are made
up of various combinations of a state board, a chief state school
officer, and a departmental staff. In five states the chief state school

officer is appointed by the governor and the state board is also appointed by the governor. The chief state school officer is appointed by the state board of education in twenty-four states, the governor appointing the state board in fourteen of these states; in nine the board is elected by the people and in one state the board is elected by the legislature. In the other twenty-one states the chief state school officer is elected by popular vote, the terms of office and methods of election varying.

The scope of authority and responsibility of state departments varies widely within the fields of public elementary and secondary education, and in other areas of education they have general responsibility for implementing educational policies and programs.

State departments are legally responsible for the general supervision of public elementary and secondary education, and for designated aspects of administration of other areas of education. They collect and report the only complete official statistics for public elementary and secondary school systems. They distribute and account for about $8 billion of state funds appropriated annually for public schools. They license teachers and other professional personnel, approve teacher-education programs, and administer special state laws of many kinds affecting education.

State departments of education also exercise critically important administrative leadership and enforcement responsibilities in the programs of instruction in the schools and in the organization and general administration of local school districts. Within constitutional limitations, state laws, and applicable federal laws and regulations, they are responsible for the administration of rapidly increasing federal funds channeled through several federal agencies for educational purposes in the states.

As a part of state government, the state department of education communicates with the governor and the legislature in regard to state organization, finance, and operation of education, covering the full scope of its activities. From its strategic position as the official state agency for education, the state department deals with other departments of state government as well as with school boards, parents, teachers, administrators, and other organized groups of citizens concerning many important aspects of education. It has cooperative relationships with public and private health, welfare, and employment agencies, with taxpayers and civic groups, with industry, labor, and agriculture, and with the general public concerning the image and specific effectiveness of education in the state.

Just as state departments of education have varying administrative structures and varying amounts of authority, they operate at varying degrees of effectiveness and public acceptance. No one of them, however, is carrying out its important functions as well as those functions deserve to be carried out, nor as well as they must be carried out.

Commissioner Keppel has said:

Often they [state departments] are understaffed, underfinanced, overworked, and so pinned down by administrative detail that they are unable to devote enough time and energy to the leadership which they alone can supply.

Put very simply, the biggest problem for state departments of education is budgetary malnutrition.

To begin with, state legislatures too frequently have not wanted to produce strong state departments. Their constituents who represent small schools in rural areas attach a great deal of importance to local control which regretably often means the right to have as poor a school as patrons will permit. Urban areas likewise cherish similar affection for local control and, again, the situation unfortunately suggests a fear that "state bureaucracy" with its concern for regulatory function and minutiae may restrict their opportunities to have as good a school as their patrons are willing to provide.

Too frequently there is such a breakdown of communication between legislative and department leaders that requested appropriations or programs are suspect from the beginning. Too frequently also the departments have been preoccupied with the regulatory function and have shown antagonism toward the continuing search for new ideas and techniques. All of this has discouraged adequate financing, without which a department cannot develop a program of both breadth and depth. It cannot recruit or hold the type of personnel which is needed to perform effectively in the exacting role of state educational leadership. A first-class state education agency cannot be bought in the bargain basement. Yet, in too many instances this has been attempted.

Parenthetically, it should be stated that every state department will experience a great deal of difficulty in finding people with the necessary qualities of leadership even if it has an attractive salary schedule. But it will face frustration, rather than merely difficulty, if it tries to find such persons at the salaries most departments are compelled to pay. For these are the very leaders who are also being sought by colleges and universities, by other branches of government, and by industry.

Reference was made earlier to the call to action on the part of state departments of education, accompanied by financial assistance from Congress. To implement this Title V of the Elementary and Secondary Education Act was written. To qualify for federal assistance, the states must develop projects which propose to get at those weaknesses and imbalances which currently limit the effectiveness of state departments of education in educational leadership. Among numerous activities which establish a bench mark against which to measure important progress, each department is requested to conduct a rather extensive self-evaluation.

Since state departments of education are agencies of state government, there should be a statewide assessment and evaluation of this specialized arm of state government. Does the present structure of the state education agency provide the framework which is most conducive to the effective carrying out of the increasingly important role of state education leadership? Such assessments are now being carried on in at least the states of California, Illinois, Kansas, and Kentucky.

For many years the Council of Chief State School Officers has had a policy statement which urged the acceptance of a state structure made up of an elected board and an appointed commissioner as the most effective structure for educational leadership. However, at the 1965 meeting of this organization in Honolulu, the policy statement was challenged and deleted largely because of the belief that the decision as to type of structure was a matter of state determination to be made freely by each state.

The disavowal of this policy was no doubt a correct move. The long look will not only require an examination of the state department of education within each state but such a look will find much to be said for the structure described earlier. We have had and now have some outstanding state educational leaders who are elected. I have a most sincere respect and sincere friendliness for them as educators and as persons. At the same time I covet for them the support and assistance which can be provided by a state board made up of aggressive, courageous, dedicated lay citizens, the kind of board members who for many years have made the local American public school an effective answer to the American dream.

If this structure at the local level has been good for American education for more than a century and a half, why is it not a proper structure at the state level? If a board of education can appoint a

superintendent of schools for a community with the political complexity of Chicago, then how can one justify requiring the state
superintendent of public instruction in Illinois to stand election?
Or, put another way, should the state departments of education,
rapidly expanding both in size and importance, be a one-man operation without the counsel of a lay board responsible to the people?

The historical activities and responsibilities of state departments, while most numerous and significant, present only a prelude
to the broader and more exciting role which is now emerging. State
education departments have been given a new opportunity for
leadership—an exciting new challenge, unparalleled in our history.
Two major developments are responsible:

1. The greatly increased public commitment to education
   which is now sweeping our country;
2. The infusion of new federal funds and of new imaginative
   leadership by the federal government in helping states to
   meet urgent needs in education, including earmarked funds
   for strengthening state education agencies.

These two developments require that we take a hard look at department activities to determine where we need to add muscle, effort,
and perhaps innovations.

The function of planning has always been a key one in educational department activities. It assumes special importance in these
swiftly changing times with the constant pressures and the pulling
and hauling of many forces.

The national goal, so frequently enunciated in recent months,
of a new level of excellence in American education, points directly
to state education departments. Since states bear the legal responsibility for the provision of education, the level of excellence which
they expect of their local schools and college systems will be a major
determining factor in the quality of education which is achieved
by these institutions. Departments might well start by cooperative-
ly reassessing objectives and establishing new guidelines to moti-
vate their schools and to upgrade the attitudes and competencies
of their professional personnel, most of whom will be expected to
assume ever-stronger leadership roles.

If any one thing has emerged from all of the ferment and discussion in American education in recent years, it is the need for
innovation. In the past, innovation has not received major attention from state departments of education. Yet, the position of the
department in relation to innovation is a very critical one. State
departments of education can stymie experimentation and change

or they can release and encourage creative forces and the implementation of new ideas. In recent years, with so many new developments in our society influencing education, departments have too often been in a reactionary position of holding the line or even opposing change, rather than in the position of participation and determination in the formulation of plans and proposals for change. Each department needs a staff of specialists with ideas and the ability to translate ideas into action. Emphasis must be given to the collection of new knowledge, new ideas, and new programs. Leadership must actually be provided rather than just talked about.

The function of promoting improved administrative management in our school systems and of providing consultative services in this area is a most important one. For state departments to be delinquent in this respect is not only to deny the schools the full benefit of the funds already invested, but to lessen the chances of securing the increased investment from local, state, and federal sources which is so necessary.

The emergence of exploratory plans for a nationwide program of assessment of educational performance has underscored the importance of evaluation as a responsibility of state education departments. Whether we like it or not, the development and implementation of some kind of a nationwide assessment is inevitable. Instruments and procedures are going to be devised by someone. State departments of education will do well to take a positive attitude toward this development and participate and cooperate constructively. Such a position will provide an opportunity to give guidance and leadership in the construction of the instruments, in the wise use of the results, and in keeping the administration of the assessment program at the state and local level.

In all areas which are components of excellence in education, departments of education are uniquely qualified to serve as catalytic agents. This is particularly true in teacher education. No educational activity has so many agencies and individuals involved in a "cooperative" effort toward a common goal! New and better ways must be found in preparing teachers. New and better ways must be found to help teachers continue to grow in effectiveness. The hopes and aspirations of teacher organizations, the divergent opinions of academicians and professional educators, and the practicalities of politics all must somehow be combined together in the attempt to produce teachers good enough for tomorrow's needs. This is one of the state agencies' biggest challenges.

In summary then, state education departments should be doing those things which will reflect the growth of a nationwide concern for the quality of education, which will prepare them to deal with the critical issues of our day, and which will make them strong enough to carry out their central role with vigor and efficiency in the three-way partnership in American education.

A significant concern in the development of American education today is the determination of the appropriate role of the three levels of government—local, state, and national—in meeting the expanding needs in education.

The federal government most obviously has a legitimate stake in education. This comes from its responsibility for the general welfare, and pointedly relates to the national defense—the survival and advancement of this nation. Certainly, it is both necessary and desirable that the national government increase its concern for education. But it should be noted that this concern must always be manifested in a manner which supplements and fortifies local and state participation and control.

By Constitutional provision, by precedent, and by virtue of providing more than 90 percent of the financial support of public education, state and local governments carry the major role of senior partners. "In this nation of 50 states with vast and independent enterprise for education, the Federal government can help as a partner, and a somewhat junior partner at that," says Commissioner Keppel. To this concept many of us give hearty endorsement.

The realignment and adaptation of the roles, difficult though they may be, are necessary to the fulfillment of our goals as a democracy. State education departments will do well to consider their plans and policies for realignment and adaptation in the light of these approaches: cooperation, guidance, and vigilance. A negative attitude is not only self-defeating but harmful to the cause of education. Not only should state department officials cooperate, but they should be the leaders in cooperation—offering it positively and enthusiastically.

By anticipation and preparation they should be ready to show, with facts and studies, what the real needs are and thus provide forward-looking, professional guidance. There is a most significant role to play in helping to keep the emphasis on the educational rather than the political aspects of legislation. State departments are close enough to the local scene, yet far enough removed, to be the logical agency to coordinate nationwide objectives with local and regional realities.

It would be completely unrealistic to ignore the fact that hazards do exist in the increasing federal participation in education and in the growing emphasis on education as an instrument of national policy. Therefore, since we bear the legal responsibility for education, we must be vigilant in protecting against infringement of rightful and proper powers and functions—here again using a positive, not a negative approach. Furthermore, we must also be vigilant in protecting ourselves against ourselves, for, hard pressed as we are in these days of greater numbers and greater needs, it would be very easy for us to lapse, almost unknowingly, into a "let Uncle do it" attitude.

Our vigilance can have a very positive effect in strengthening state education departments. The people of the state need to be made to understand that their "say so" in educational matters is dependent in large measure upon the strength of their state education departments. They need to know that without that strength they may find themselves without a real voice. They need to know that their response to state-level needs in education may in large measure determine the place the state will continue to have in the federal system. Knowing these things, they can, through their legislators, provide the necessary state support to maintain the senior-partner role of local and state government.

In discussing the matter of role clarification, Commissioner James E. Allen, Jr. of New York summed it up quite succinctly in an oral presentation to the Council of Chief State School Officers in Honolulu on November 12, 1965, when he said:

In this era, we have, both as individual states and on a nationwide basis, an opportunity to demonstrate that our capabilities are equal to our responsibilities, to show our willingness and readiness to make necessary adaptations and adjustments, and to justify the continuing power of the strategic position we occupy. The leadership of the states—particularly of the state education departments—is being tried and tested as never before. If we are not willing to make the necessary changes, and to do what is needed to make ourselves strong, we could well find that our generation of Chief State School Officers will go down in history as the one which allowed the states to lose their position of power in the making of educational policy in America.

George Brain, President of American Association of School Administrators, in speaking to state boards and state departments of education in Portland, Oregon, October 14, 1965, threw at us this challenge:

Unless state departments of education light up these issues by focusing knowledge, wisdom, and experience on them, the light of public understanding will be so diffuse that its beam will be too weak to penetrate the darkness of confusion, distrust, and misunderstanding that will arise. If that occurs, then strangers to the education profession will clamor to grasp the switch, shouting a solution that does not reflect the public interest, the pupil's interest, or the educator's interest.

Should such a turn of events take place it would be a tragedy—a national disaster. This need not take place. It must not take place. If those of us at the state level assume our role of leadership with energy, enthusiasm, competence and professional dedication, the 1960's will be written into the pages of history as the decade when state departments of education faced up to their responsibilities and won.

Roald F. Campbell

THE CONTROL OF PUBLIC EDUCATION*

There are in the United States some thirty thousand school districts, and in these districts there are about one hundred thousand elementary schools and thirty thousand high schools. For each district there is a board of education and one or more teachers. In at least half of the districts there is also a superintendent of schools, and for many of the larger districts a number of other school administrators. But who really controls these schools? The citizens? The boards? The administrators? The teachers?

I am using the word *control* to mean more than legal control; *influence* might be a better term. My purpose is to suggest how decisions about American schools get made. I would first like to indicate briefly the kinds of controls, or influences, that appear to affect American schools, then note how the larger society attempts to shape the school, and, in turn, suggest how the school mediates such influences.

KINDS OF CONTROL

The controls or influences that affect schools may be grouped into three major categories. First, there is the legal structure. Despite the fact that the Constitution does not mention education, the federal government, chiefly through the Congress and the courts, has always exerted some influence on the schools. Every state constitution deals with schools specifically; in each state there is also a body of statutory law regarding education; and each state

*Adapted from an article by Dr. Campbell previously published in *Elementary School Journal*, Vol. 65, No. 3, University of Chicago Press, 1964.

legislature is, in a sense, the big school board. There is some justification in the contention that there are fifty school systems in this
country. In nearly every state, however, the actual operation of
schools has been delegated to local school districts. There are other
structural refinements, but this is the essential picture.

What of the actors within this structure? For the sake of
simplicity, let us mention only those in the local school district.
There is first the board of education, usually elected by the people
of the district. In legal terms, the board is the administrative body
for the district, but the board operates under many constraints,
including state law and local tradition. Moreover, most boards
employ an administrative officer, most commonly called a superintendent, and he tends to influence the board as well as do its
bidding. But school cannot be kept without teachers, and teachers
individually and collectively determine in large part what the school
is and what it does.

These official actors—board members, administrators, and
teachers—important as they are, do not perform in a social vacuum.
Thus we must say a word about the social matrix within which the
school operates. At the local or school-district level this leads us to
such considerations as the power structure of the community.
Whether one accepts the reputational approach of Hunter, the
pluralistic approach of Dahl, or some combination of the two, it is
clear that lay citizens, at least some lay citizens, have considerable
voice in school affairs, including the allocation of resources to support schools.

Nor does school government, any more than any other government, operate without the pressures of special-interest groups. Some
of these groups, such as parent-teacher associations and the League
of Women Voters, are usually disposed to support school programs,
while others, such as taxpayers' associations and militant civil-
rights groups, often feel that school programs go too far and not
far enough.

But special-interest groups are seldom a local phenomenon
only. The position of the interest group on a particular school
program—whether expressed by chambers of commerce, farm bu-
reaus, the John Birch Society, or the local education association—is
often an expression espoused by the national organization, which
has expended great effort to keep the locals in line. In the social
matrix as in the legal structure, schools are not controlled locally;
they are a part of the larger society.

Even this sketchy treatment of schools suggests that controls are numerous, that they are formal and informal, legal and extra-legal, covert and overt. While some controls reside within the school organization, others appear to reside outside the organization. For the school is a subsystem of a larger social system, a relationship not always clearly perceived and one to which we now turn.

SOCIETY AND THE SCHOOL

The controls that the larger society exerts over the schools appear to fall into three major categories. These may be identified as the constraints imposed by the traditions and values of society, the economic resources made available by society for the schools, and the governmental structures established by society through which schools must operate.

Traditions and Values

Two traditions or values appear to be particularly relevant here. The first might be called a faith in education and the second a strong tradition of localism. Faith in education, or perhaps more specifically in schooling, has long been characteristic of the American people. The establishment of schools began early in Massachusetts, spread to the other colonies, and continued with our independence and development as a nation. To begin with, the common school included only elementary instruction, but in time the high school was included, and subsequent to the passage of the Morrill Act in 1862, college opportunity was extended to a large portion of the college-age group.

This faith in education was probably born of our independence, our lack of an elite class, our decades of experience with an expanding frontier, our abundance of resources, and our conviction that one man is as good as another. Egalitarianism became a dominant value in our national development, and the school was seen as one way of giving expression to that value. Adherence to this value has always given us some trouble, for people are not equal in ability nor do they profit equally from the same kind of educational experience, but we have chosen to err on the side of Jacksonian instead of Jeffersonian democracy.

The belief in the efficacy of education as a way of meeting our social and economic problems still persists. When we have unemployment, we tend to establish retraining programs. When we fall behind in space technology, we get congressional provisions for augmenting science and mathematics instruction. When juvenile delinquency increases, we look to the schools for remedial measures. This great faith in education may at times retard instead of advance the solution of our problems. Too much reliance on the school may mean too little reliance on the family, the courts, and other agencies of our society.

But the belief in schools persists. Education is valued, although educators may not be. People may become disenchanted with a particular school or school program, but they tend to retain a faith in education as the open sesame to personal and social progress. Little wonder that the civil-rights movement has tended to center on the schools. Negroes, believe, as other Americans do, that free access to good schools and colleges will permit the Negro to improve his lot both socially and economically.

This basic belief in education means that the people strive to support schools and colleges. It also means that, when schools and colleges do not appear to be operating in the best interests of society, people intervene and attempt to change their operation. Citizen influence on the schools is usually a sign of concern, not lack of faith.

The people of America also have a long tradition of localism. This too is probably a product of our settlement and our long frontier experience. We believed firmly that the federal government should have limited powers and that other powers should be reserved to the states or to the people. The phrase "to the people" was not an idle one. There was a disposition to rely on government for no more than was necessary and to expect the people as individual citizens to do the rest.

Moreover, if local government could perform a particular function, that function was not shifted to the government of the colony or the state. Thus, in Massachusetts the towns were early required to support schools. Many towns failed to meet the requirement, but the concept was one of local action, not one of colonial provision. This tradition of localism was carried across the country as people migrated from the eastern seaboard to the West. Again, the frontier society reinforced individual initiative and local effort.

The American tradition of localism, so appropriate in our early history, has been identified with private enterprise, chiefly by the business groups of our society. Anyone who does not subscribe to such a view is almost seen as a subversive. But the frontier society is gone, and in its place we have an urban, industrial society which poses many problems that are not local in nature. Most of our major problems such as poverty, unemployment, civil rights, mass transportation, communication, world peace, and educational opportunity require local, state, national and even worldwide effort if they are to be solved. It is this shift in the nature of our problems that is behind the growth of federalism.

Recognition of this fact is essential if the educational problems of the nation are to be solved. Many localities cannot provide educational opportunity for the children, the youths, and the adults of their communities; they must have state assistance. In turn, some states cannot or will not provide adequate educational opportunity for the people within their boundaries; the only alternative is federal assistance. Our tradition of localism provides the basis for resisting these solutions, but gradually that tradition is being modified.

I have dealt with only two traditions or values of the American people, but even this brief treatment suggests that these deep-seated attitudes influence the schools of the nation. Those who would change the educational program may find their efforts blocked because the people perceive such changes to be contrary to the education they have cherished. Those who would use federal aid to help alleviate local inadequacies in the schools may encounter resistance, for again many perceive such aid to be contrary to the American way.

Economic Resources

Schools require economic support. While money expended is not a perfect measure of the quality of an educational program, it is probably the best single index of quality. Expenditures vary greatly among school districts. The differences are due in part to the uneven distribution of economic resources. One district may have many pupils to be placed in school and may depend for its assessed valuation entirely on low- and medium-priced residences. A second district may have few pupils and enjoy an assessed valuation made up in major part by a large industrial complex. The alternatives that confront these two districts are very different.

To be sure, state foundation programs often contain an equalization provision designed to reduce the differences suggested here. But the level of state equalization is often very low. In Illinois, for instance, the foundation program guarantees each district annually $252 per pupil in average daily attendance. The average expenditure per pupil for the state is about $500, and in some districts expenditures are as much as $1,000 per pupil annually. A very high tax rate in the poorest districts will not yield enough money to permit those districts to go much beyond the expenditure level guaranteed by the state. This condition has very direct effects on the schools.

But the economy is called upon to support services other than schools. Municipal government, police and fire protection, roads, sewers, water, and other services must also be provided. Often the school bond issue must compete with the bond issue of the sanitary district. Salary increases for teachers may be caught up in the issue of salary increases for firemen and policemen. In new suburban communities, particularly, many of these demands are concurrent. In these cases, it is not only a question of the level of economic resources, but of the allocation of these resources; and decisions on allocation will have direct import for the schools.

In the short run, the level and the allocation of economic resources in a school district may be looked upon as a given factor that affects in some measure what might be done in that school district. In the long run, level of education and economic resources are interdependent. Education becomes the chief vehicle for creating human capital, which in turn affects the total economy. A skilled labor force is as necessary to a healthy economy as natural resources are.

This interdependence between level of education and productivity is difficult to determine at a local or even at a state level. In economic terms, the nation tends to be the unit, and in many instances the economy is subject to worldwide influences. People with high-level work skills are drawn to those centers in the nation where these skills are in demand. In turn, production is increased, and the benefits of the increased production tend to be absorbed by the entire nation. Neither the migration of workers nor the spread of benefits works perfectly, but both processes go on.

The integrated nature of the economy represents another reason for providing economic resources for the schools on more than a local basis. State aid and particularly federal aid can help spread the benefits of the economy over the nation so that the educational level of the entire nation can make its best contribution to the economy. This concept is not fully accepted by all groups in American society, but continued movement toward acceptance appears likely.

In the meantime, economic resources available from local sources, from existing state sources, and from existing federal sources will continue to affect the nature and level of the school program which any school district can mount.

Governmental Structure

Governmental arrangments in this country are numerous and overlapping. A single small school district may overlap eight or ten other units of government. These units may include one or more villages, a fire district, a water district, a sanitary district, a recreation district, a toll road, and other special-purpose governments. For a citizen to participate responsibly in such an environment is almost impossible. Perhaps multiplicity of government has contributed to the indifference many people exhibit toward government.

The school district itself is an example of special government. When the government of the school district must be conducted within numerous overlapping jurisdictions, complications ensue for the school as well as for the citizen. Village zoning ordinances, for instance, may contain provisions that ignore possible implications for the school-age population and thus for the schools. Two villages in the same school district may have quite different provisions on building permits, street construction, or fire protection. Or, two school districts may be located in the same municipality, one district embracing largely the business section and thus having high assessed valuations, the other district limited to residential property and thus having low assessed valuations. In any case, many special governments and frequent overlapping jurisdictions often affect school-district operation.

But governmental structure affects schools even more directly. Some structures are relatively open to the expression of local aspirations for education. In such structures, the board of education and the people can exercise some control over the local school. Other structures are relatively closed, and neither the board of education nor the people of the local district can exercise much of an option regarding education. In the closed situations most decisions are made at the county or the state level. This condition tends to pull all educational programs to the mean, lifting the bottom programs and reducing the top programs. Thus, the level of government at which educational decisions are made affects the nature of the school program.

Many of our governmental arrangements are obsolete. We have too many school districts, too many counties, too many villages, and too many other governmental units. Moreover, we appear to have too much special government for a single purpose and too little general government for many purposes. Special government has led to overlapping jurisdictions that add to the difficulty of all government.

But to change these arrangements is difficult. Our tradition of localism supports obsolescent practices. Often politicians would lose their jobs if more rational governmental units were established; units with high assessed valuations do not wish to be combined with units with low assessed valuations. In short, we find it easier to continue doing what we have been doing than to change. This resistance to change affects school-district reorganization as well as the relationship the schools have to all other governmental units.

THE SCHOOL AND SOCIETY

It is clear that the larger society creates the school, imposes its values upon the school, decides what resources the school may use, and prescribes the way the school is to be governed. But the school or school district has ways of resisting or mediating these controls. The bureaucratic nature of organizations, the professionalism of teachers, and the leadership of the administrator represent these countervailing forces.

Organizational Characteristics

Organizations per se have a being, a nature, that affects the people who are members of the organizations and, in a sense, helps insulate the organization from the larger world. Organizations develop bureaucratic characteristics such as large size, specialization of work, hierarchical authority structure, reliance on rules and regulations, and personal detachment.

Schools, like other bureaucracies, have a hierarchical authority structure. Authority proceeds from the board of education to the superintendent, to the principal, to the teacher. While many people lament these hierarchical arrangements, no adequate alternative has yet been evolved. There are, however, wide differences in how the hierarchical structure is now employed.

In some school situations, almost complete reliance is placed on the flow of authority. Thus, the board directs the superintendent, the superintendent directs the principal, and the principal directs the teacher. While the formal structure permits and accepts this state of affairs, complete reliance on such an arrangement may produce a number of dysfunctions. For instance, giving and taking orders may prevent the development and consideration of ideas, organization members may devise informal means of "beating the system," and potentially able contributors may develop indifference toward the organization.

In some school systems, the authority dimension is mediated by recognition of the competence of staff members. While authority flows down, influence flows both ways. Teachers make suggestions to principals, principals to superintendents, and superintendents to school boards. Communication is down, up, and across. These organizations have an open climate. Such a climate may contribute to greater productivity in the organization and to greater satisfaction on the part of organization members, both of which can be important influences on schools.

Organizations have built-in protection against the larger society. Personal detachment, reliance on rules and regulations, and hierarchical structure all provide protection against the larger world. In a school, for instance, a case can usually be made against granting a request to a particular parent on the grounds that similar requests could not be granted to other parents; in other words, parents must be treated in a universalistic, not in a particularistic, manner. Or, school personnel may take refuge behind the rules and regulations and maintain that the request of the parent is against the policy of the school. Or, should either of these devices fail, the hierarchical structure can be employed. The principal can suggest that the granting of a request is beyond his prerogative; that the parent may see the superintendent if he wishes to do so.

For the parent to go to the superintendent takes effort. In the meantime, the principal may alert the superintendent to the impending visit of the parent and make a case against the granting of the request. When the parent finally gets to see the superintendent, he may encounter the same arguments he did with the principal: the need to keep the matter in a universalistic context, prohibition by the policies of the board of education, and, as a final resort, an appointment with the board of education. Little wonder that parents and other citizens feel at times that they cannot influence the schools, which presumably are public and for which they pay taxes. Yet, few would maintain that schools of the larger society could operate with any effectiveness if any parent at any time could penetrate the organization and alter its operation.

Professionalism

Still another influence on the school is what may be called professionalism. The teacher who would be a professional finds he must cope with a growing body of knowledge in one or more content areas as well as with increasing knowledge about the teaching and learning process. Teachers are tending to become more proficient in both of these bodies of knowledge. School systems are recognizing the growing importance of in-service education programs for teachers. Many of these programs use the services of university scholars, and teachers in schools tend to identify with the professors who represent their respective disciplines.

The joining of school and college scholars has been particularly characteristic of the national curriculum programs in science, mathematics, and foreign languages, a movement now being extended to other fields. Thus, high-school physics teachers were teamed with university physicists in the Physical Science Study Committee, a project with headquarters at Massachusetts Institute of Technology. The relationship of high-school and college instructors in a particular discipline was further enhanced through the year-long and summer institutes organized for high-school teachers on many university campuses.

Recent devices for increasing the professional expertise of teachers tend to represent national programs. Thus, there have been national programs in biological science, chemistry, mathematics, foreign languages, guidance, social studies, and English. While these developments have been influenced by the larger society, particularly through congressional support of the National Science Foundation and its curriculum programs, the programs have also contributed toward the establishment of teachers as a distinctive group in the larger world, with greater consciousness of their own expertise and their own values.

Professionalism has a way of resisting intervention from the larger society. For instance, some school districts have withstood pressure from lay citizens to adopt an all-out phonics approach in the teaching of reading. In the process, the teachers and the administrators in the school system marshalled evidence from members of their professional groups across the nation to support their current practice. Citizens were told that this was a professional matter, that the evidence was fairly clear, and that only the professionals should make such a decision. Moreover, as the professionalism of teachers grows, the validity of such an argument will increase.

The increased professionalism of teachers has another kind of relevance for the school district. There is a growing conflict between professional and hierarchical control of schools. Obviously, the administrator cannot become expert in every content area of the curriculum. Thus, in some ways, he is not prepared to make decisions about many matters that are central to the school program. The board of education, composed of laymen, is even less well prepared to decide what and how to teach. Only teachers have the expertise required for some way of modifying hierarchical control so as to use the expertise of the professional. This problem presents one of the real challenges in school organizations.

Leadership of Administrators

The school can also resist the larger society through the leadership of the administrator. Some administrators do little more than maintain an organization. Others affect some changes in the goals, programs, and procedures of an organization. The latter activity represents leadership. While changes in goals, programs, or procedures may be expressed within the organization, their legitimation must reside in the world surrounding the organization. Thus, the administrator who would lead is required to stimulate his staff as well as to convince his public.

The administrator who would lead works with both the professional members of the organization and with the lay citizens, especially when goals and direction are involved. For instance, to expand and reshape vocational education would represent a new direction for many school districts. Such an idea is likely to be viewed with suspicion by many school people. Those in vocational education may be reluctant to alter well-established programs. Those out of vocational education may feel that a less-important part of the program is now getting undue emphasis. Lay citizens, too, may look on the idea with little favor, particularly citizens of middle- and upper-middle-class status who are much more interested in the college-preparatory programs of the school.

The prospects of getting approval for a new emphasis in vocational education under these circumstances are not great. Yet the facts cry out for such a change. The occupational structure has undergone and is continuing to undergo change. Since almost all unskilled jobs are being automated out of existence, many unskilled workers will have to be trained to do skilled or technical jobs, or they will be unemployable. The administrator who has some grasp of such facts and who is convinced that the school should play a part in helping society meet its problems will try to get professional school workers and lay citizens to face the problem. If the administrator succeeds in getting some change of position on the part of the staff and the public, he will have exerted some leadership. With substantial agreement on the new goal, many lesser decisions to implement it can be made.

In this illustration the traditions and values of many people in the larger world precluded, at first, their approval of a revamped vocational educational program. A more realistic view of the larger world and perhaps some restructuring of their values permitted them to accept the idea. The administrator was not resisting the larger world. Rather, he was calling attention to neglected aspects of the larger world and insisting that the school could and should do something to improve conditions as they were emerging.

The administrator who would lead must be armed with both facts and values. He stands little chance of convincing his professional colleagues or his lay public if he has no factual support for his case. But besides having a command of the facts, the administrator who leads must believe that the school has a role to play in meeting a social problem. Armed with both information and commitment the administrator will then need to use every ethical procedure at his command if he is also to lead.

By way of summary, may I note that the larger society tries to shape the school by imposing its traditions and values, by controlling the resources made available to the school, and through the governmental arrangements established for the school. The school does not simply accept these impositions; countervailing forces are marshalled to mediate the impingements of the larger world. These forces include the bureaucratic nature of the school, the growing professionalism of teachers, and the leadership of the administrators. In this interaction between society and the school, bureaucracy gives the school some protection from immediate access by every subpublic in the larger world, and professionalism marshalls an expertise not possessed by the larger world, but administrative leadership is required to help the larger world reconceive its expectations for the school. It is this interaction which gives us hope that the school will not only mirror society but help to improve it.

William J. Ellena

MAN AND THE DAY AFTER TOMORROW

There is an inevitable divergence, attributable perhaps to the imperfections of the human mind, between the world as it really is and the world as men perceive it. As long as our perceptions are reasonably close to reality, it is possible for us to act upon problems and issues in a rational and appropriate manner. But when our perceptions fail to keep pace with events, when we refuse to believe something because it displeases or frightens us, or is simply startlingly unfamiliar, then it seems to me that the gap between fact and perception becomes a great chasm and action becomes irrelevant and irrational. Therefore, before looking at man's tomorrows, I think we must first assess our perceptions of today—a galloping age of technology.

Recently Margaret Mead, the famous sociologist-anthropologist, stated that one of the truly great problems in education comes about because of the rather fantastic change in the rate of change. She says this is what necessitates a break with the past—a change from the vertical to the lateral transmission of knowledge. We might very well ask ourselves, "Just how diligently have we sought to understand the scope and magnitude of the scientific and technological change which is sweeping our nation and the world, and how much effort have we really made to bring into a clear focus some of the implications of this change for education?"

To help us understand this matter of the change in the rate of change, let us consider a simple and homely illustration. Suppose we say that mankind has had 50,000 years of recorded history. In order to bring this into a comprehensible span of time, let's compress the 50,000 years into fifty years. If we accept this scale, then we stopped being cavemen about ten years ago. Five years ago, pictorial writing was invented. Two years ago, Christianity was born. Fifteen months ago we had the first printing press in Western Europe. Ten days ago electricity was put into practical use. Yesterday, the airplane flew for the first time in the morning and the radio was invented last night. Television came into being early this morning and the commercial jet was invented since I started talking.

Now, speed is a good indicator of technological growth. So let us take the speed that a man can travel as an index of our technological progress. How fast could a man travel 50,000 years ago? His top speed was probably as fast as a horse could take him. And the top speed of a horse was the fastest that man could travel right up to the year 1829. In the year 1829, however, the tempo of things picked up a little. A contest took place in England between a steam locomotive on the Liverpool-Manchester Railroad and a man on a race horse. And for the first time, with 49,870 years of recorded history behind him, man moved faster in a machine of his own making than he had previously been able to by natural means.

Then, in 1910, the U. S. Army let a contract for the building of our first military airplane. The only specification in the contract was that it be able to fly at least 40 miles per hour. Upon its completion, it actually flew 42 miles per hour. In 1925, the winner of the Indianapolis Speedway Race exceeded 100 miles per hour. And toward the end of World War II, 470 miles per hour was such a fantastic speed in flying that it was kept top secret for months.

Then something happened! For almost 40,000 years, man had virtually crawled about this earth with comparatively little change in speed—then he suddenly exploded. In 1945, he broke the sound barrier and within twelve years he had machines in operation that were traveling 18,000 miles per hour. His speed graph had suddenly taken a right angle turn. It was just that sudden. Interestingly enough, if we trace the history of events in other fields, we would find, with few exceptions, a high correlation between them and the curve just mentioned. Yes, 1945 was the year. That was the year of the big change—the year progress exploded. That was the year that somebody threw away the blueprint of the world—the world in which we used to live, the world in which we were born, reared, and educated. The old world has literally ceased to exist and there is every likelihood that change will continue to accelerate. For example, one-half of all monies spent on research and development in the history of the United States has been expended within the past eight years.

Now surely, anyone who dares predict what lies ahead in this kaleidoscopic, rapidly moving society does so with much foolhardy daring and a very strong likelihood of seeing many of his predictions go awry. Yet, recognizing the obstacles, perhaps we could try.

Good education, generally speaking, reflects the spirit of the times; it gives the learner the power to understand the world in which he lives; it seeks to engender the imaginative and creative quality of mind needed to envision a world with its blueprint still in formation.

Even casual observers note that the world in general is in a violent state of revolution. Earth-shaking events and movements have caused the American people to become insecure, if not frightened. The upsurge of worldwide nationalism rampant in colonial and undeveloped areas, together with a deep-seated faith that a better life can be found, must be recognized and respected by America. The bitter debate of conflicting ideologies the world over threatens to burst into violence. The word megaton now takes on awesome meaning. Hopes that conflicts between nations can be settled by reason and peaceful cooperation fluctuate upward and downward.

Occasionally people who purport to be scholars cite, as evidence that man will always have trouble living with man, the first stanza of a famous poem written by Kipling:

> "Oh, East is East and West is West,
> And never the twain shall meet,
> Till earth and sky stand presently
> At God's great judgment seat."

The next time you hear this stanza cited you might recall the second stanza of the very same poem:

> "But there is neither East nor West,
> Border, nor breed, nor birth
> When two strong men stand face to face,
> Though they come from the ends of the earth."

The shifting population of the United States; the interdependence among all of our citizens which has developed as a result of modern transportation and instantaneous communication; the interrelatedness of an economy which is no longer local in scope and character; and changing social viewpoints of our own dynamic nation of free people are mere forerunners to the changing scenes among other people of the world. Presently there is no world organization, or voice, or combination of voices with enough strength and wisdom to coordinate the efforts of the many nations that are trying to adjust themselves to neighborly living.

Abundance and scarcities exist side by side. Those who do *not* have a reasonable amount of food and shelter are conscious that the world can be made to produce enough for them to have their share. Fears have created a demand for mighty military preparation. Just when man's producing powers make it possible to eliminate waste and release human energy for the cultural purposes and peaceful forms of service, his fears demand military expenditures that consume an inordinate portion of his productive power.

The Cold War—the one in which we find ourselves at the moment—has already had some profound effects on the American people. For example, one of its most significant effects has been an inversion of priorities. It has consumed money and time and talent that could otherwise have been used to build schools and homes and hospitals, to remove the blight of ugliness that is spreading over many of the cities and highways in our land, and to overcome the poverty and hopelessness that afflict the lives of one-fifth of the people in an otherwise affluent society. It has put a very high premium on avoiding innovation at home because new programs involve controversy as well as expense, and it is felt that we cannot afford domestic division at a time when external challenge requires us to maintain the highest possible degree of national unity.

Let us turn now from this very brief and cursory view of some of the conditions that exist at the moment to a look at some of the conditions that are likely to prevail in this country within the next two decades.

By that time, automation in industry will have been greatly accelerated. This will have some profound effects, not all of them anticipated. For example, despite notable advances in the formal rights of Negroes since the Supreme Court decision of 1954, employment prospects for Negroes are actually declining, and they are declining at an accelerating rate. The causes of this are now twofold —inadequate education and the spread of automation. Factory and service jobs, which have been the principal sources of Negro employment, are the very jobs that are being eliminated by automation at rates estimated to be from 20,000 to 40,000 per week.

The general education and technical skills demanded of the men and women who operate our industries and business places will

have greatly increased over present requirements. The whole problem of managing production, distributing goods, and accounting
for them will increase mightily and will call for further education.
Mechanization in the production of goods will increase to the point
where America will either have half the adult population unemployed, together with useless surpluses, or the people will demand
a great increase in services. It is predicted that the latter will occur.
Furthermore, it seems as if the unskilled man of the future will
have few outlets for his energies and will surely be unemployed.
Competitive machine power has made the labors of the unskilled
prohibitive in costs.

It must be predicted as well that the world will be largely
demilitarized. Peace is the only way by which men can have any
real chance of existing on this earth. Perhaps mankind will heed
the words of the recently deposed ruler of the Soviet Union when
he said, "If all the nuclear weapons were touched off, the world
would be in such a state that the survivors would envy the dead."
The only war that can possibly exist is a cold war. But it will rage
in full fury. Competition will be in the areas of values, cultural
attainments, economy, education, and social and governmental theories. Ways not even contemplated at the present time will be
devised for men to resolve their differences and for nations to settle
disputes in a reasonable, peaceful fashion. The energy which now
drives our submarines under the ice at the North Pole will be in
general use, bringing undreamed-of comforts and blessings, but at
the same time disrupting great areas of economy. Other new forms
of energy, too, will be the slave of man. Problems of adjustment
will be big and complex as we shift to new sources of energy. Whole
population groups will be forced to change occupations, ways of
living, and places of residence.

Americans particularly will develop culturally to the point
where higher values will be placed on art, literature, drama, music,
education, and health services. The eternal search for material
goods already in abundance will diminish, thus removing old fears
of survival and establishing new priorities of values. More citizens
will begin to require more in the ways of services. Large blocks of
manpower will be shifted from the production of material goods to
the production of services, or the rendering of cultural, aesthetic,
and spiritual help to our people. Thus, professions will tend to
multiply.

Ethnic and religious diversity, of which the United States has
always had a generous share, will be multiplied over and over.

Instead of facing the relatively easy task of developing understanding and respect between Catholic, Protestant, and Jew, the citizens of the United States, being in everyday contact with Moslems, Hindus, Buddhists, and followers of many other great religions, must develop understanding, tolerance, and respect for them all. The American concept of independence in thought and worship will, of necessity, become the rule of the world.

Economic interdependence, a greatly improved communication system, and rapid transportation will tend to destroy the independent community in America as we have known it. Larger and more complex communities will form. Small political governmental units will disappear rapidly. The county and the New England town will be greatly enlarged or eliminated. In all probability, rockets will be used for long-distance travel within the environment of the earth and men will travel in outer space in vehicles controlled by the occupants. Most diseases now commonly known will be eradicated, but the biggest development perhaps will be in the field of emotional or mental infirmity. Psychiatry will come into its own and the emotional terrors which rend men's souls will be conquered. And there is a possibility that children born with seeming mental handicaps will, through new discoveries and applications, be brought to normality.

The complexity and the technical specializations of such a society suggest the likelihood and necessity for teams of persons to work as a unit, while capitalizing on individual competence as a cooperative part of the total galaxy of skills and understandings needed in a great new world. Some of the most challenging problems which will confront mankind will be in the fields of government and human relations, including the value systems of different cultures. Here the emphasis will be placed on achieving a better understanding of man himself through psychology, philosophy, history, anthropology, and the creative arts. Education will be led by teams composed of representatives from many disciplines.

The citizens of the United States will have taken important steps toward guaranteeing the place of the individual in self-government. Because of the complexity of governmental problems and the increasing need for prompt decisive action, government officials, serving the people, will be required to make more decisions and be responsible for these decisions. This requirement will demand a greater amount of education and competence on the part of our public officials and more intelligent voting on the part of all citizens.

Television will become such a significant force in the formation of public opinion, in the dissemination of information, and in education that it will have to be controlled to a greater degree by the public. Possibly, many aspects will have to become publically financed and as completely publically controlled and operated as are the public schools, the courts, and the postal service. Since television and radio broadcasting transcend local and state education administrative units, the danger of leaving these important media of communication in the hands of individuals or groups that neither feel a responsibility to the public nor can be controlled by the public will become apparent and will demand public policy. The application of the fundamental principles of public policy to the control and use of radio and television in education constitutes a problem which the American people must soon face.

Without question, a stronger international organization will be developed to coordinate the relationships of people everywhere. This does not mean that the loyalty which now exists within nations will be weakened or destroyed. But it means that another loyalty will operate alongside that of patriotism to one's own country. No greater spark of hope exists today than the development of such a pattern of international cooperation. The violent upsurge of nationalism found in all new nations, big and little, unless tempered and accompanied by an understanding of interdependence and inter-relatedness—the brotherhood of man—may prove to be an evil of devastating proportions.

Communication between people will probably be the most difficult of all international problems. A common international language will be accepted.

Further, it would seem that there is every likelihood that a far larger percentage of our minerals, our food, and our raw products will come from the sea. Herein will be one of the truly great commercial developments of the next two or three decades.

The weather, particularly precipitation, will be under the control of man. Deserts can and will be made to bloom. Meteorologists are suggesting the possibility of ridding ourselves of the harm inflicted on people by hurricanes and tornadoes. To do this, mankind undoubtedly will develop means by which hurricanes can be identified in their infancy, while it is still possible to cope with their awesome power. Let us take a look at the power in a hurricane. Imagine, if you will, the energy involved when an automobile is moving down a highway at 75 miles an hour. Now, imagine a cake of ice one mile square and 65 feet deep, moving down the same highway at 75 miles an hour. Now, imagine a cake of ice that is 10 miles wide on a side, 65 feet deep, moving at the same speed down a highway. Lastly, imagine a cake of ice that is 50 miles long on each side and is 65 feet deep, moving down the highway at a speed of 75 miles an hour. That is the amount of energy in a typical mature hurricane. Thus, you can readily see why it is necessary, with the limited means that we have at our disposal, to identify hurricanes when they are little fellows so that we can have some hope of coping with them.

And what are the implications of all this for education? How will education adust to meet these changes? Here are some guesses.

American education has been dynamic and flexible enough to initiate change and to cope with change in the past. Education must continue to do so in the future. The accent we have placed in the past and are continuing to place on every individual and his full development as a *free operator* will probably be the most important factor in adequately preparing citizens for the next half century. This is our "secret" weapon. Equal opportunity for all has been a basic goal of American education for three generations. But in the implementation of this basic principle, our practice falls far short of our aim. On the present scene considerable retreat can be observed. A false philosophy of saving the best and shooting the rest has for a short time been in the ascendancy. It is maintained by a few national figures who pose as sages that some individuals are more worthy of society's concern than others. The need for diversity of interests and varied intellectual power and special creativity is overlooked, and a common mold seems to be proposed as a sound educational pattern.

The philosophical commitment to equality of opportunity forces teachers to face the problem of individual differences. However, some of the loudest supporters of the doctrine of individual differences and the importance of individual initiative contradict themselves by advocating rigid conformity in school curricula. But the values of America and the professional competence of the teaching profession will, within a few years, quiet those voices and restore faith in the essential worth of each individual.

Some speakers and writers make the assumption today that equality of opportunity requires the sacrificing of excellence. A few persons push the idea that we cannot *afford both quality and quantity in education*. Indeed, some say the two are contradictory, and we cannot have both. Since these attacks are now and will continue to be covered under a variety of cloaks of respectability, including "academic" respectability, the appeal is all the more enticing to the unwary. But teachers and parents are learning to expect and to detect these attacks on fundamental educational values. The American concept that each human being is uniquely valuable and should be developed to full potential will be as logically, as sensibly, and as unswervingly supported in the cultural era which we now see appearing on the horizon as it has been in the ideals of our past history.

If we stop reacting as if every scratch were an incurable wound, and if we are not frightened into imbalance by the technology and fears of our times, we will continue to teach an understanding of and a devotion to the principles fought for by American patriots since the days of the Mayflower Compact, the Connecticut Fundamental Orders, the Constitution with amendments, and the Gettysburg Address. New emphases on these basic concepts and values in our present educational program will enable our young people to do what must be done. We must interpret these basic democratic principles to millions of non-Americans who are more interested in Jefferson, Lincoln, Mark Twain, and Leonard Bernstein than they are in Dr. Teller or Admiral Rickover. American dreams and American humanistic goals must be reversed and there must be skill to interpret them everywhere if the battle for free men is to be won. This will be an overriding purpose of the educational program of the future.

Standards of professional preparation and the competence of the educational staff will improve. At the present time superintendents must have at least two years of graduate work in a well-recognized college or university to be admitted to full status in their national association. The future will call for more graduate work. The standard and qualifications of teachers have risen at a phenomenal rate since 1945 and will continue upward. Periods of preparation are not only longer, but the quality of work has improved with strengthened scholarship. Preparation for teaching, like the education of other professional workers, will be greatly improved by the end of the century.

Few people would argue with the fact that most textbooks become obsolete in approximately five years. Teachers, too, may become obsolete in five years unless something happens to them during that period. In fact, if we really took a hard look at the cost to society when we retain obsolete teachers, we know it would be much cheaper if we retired teachers after five years unless they are involved in continuing in-service education.

During the next two decades, there may be another new development on the scene. Teachers and school administrators are going to have Thursdays off for thinking. This is a development that has been needed for a long, long time. A school administrator especially must find some time when he can think, when he can dream, when he can envision some of the problems and opportunities confronting the school district.

Furthermore, unless we backtrack on what we know about human beings, unless we are frightened away from our best practices, we will continue to consider the interests, the emotions, and the mental and physical health of children and youth important factors in intellectual development. Without emotional balance, physical health and strength, belief in and understanding of human values, as well as intellectual and technical power, the American of tomorrow will fail. But the excitement over passing examinations based on specific factual information, making a good showing on memory quizzes, and striving for so-called excellence in mastery of content of primary interest to adults and testmakers outside the school system may destroy this balance of education. Herein lie the obstacles that sensible laymen must help the teaching profession overcome—and soon.

We established the universal school system to prepare citizens for a free society, a society where all men had the privilege of exercising freedom and of making free choices. Our school system was designed to produce men of judgment. Controversial issues and difficult problems have not upset our people to the point of *revolution* and violent overthrow. Schools have had a curriculum from the kindergarten to senior high designed to develop this kind of citizen-thinkers. The search for truth, the right to question and dissent, respect for nonconformity—all of which are values that helped make America strong and unique—will receive new emphasis in our schools. Free choice and the power to make sound judgments will either be re-emphasized in these coming years, or self-government and freedom of choice will disappear and the death knell of America's dream will sound.

Outmoded concepts relative to the operation of schools will be changed drastically to meet the demands of the emerging, changing world. Asserting local autonomy, independent little islands of school systems with iron curtains pulled tightly around themselves, controlled by boards of education acting like ostriches with heads in the sand, sometimes try to solve problems which are created by forces *outside* the district and which have solutions only on the *outside*. Dependence on old sources of school revenue for school finance is a good example of an obsolescent approach which the years ahead will change. Even the curriculum is not confined to local needs as it was fifty years ago.

If by A.D. 2000 America has mastered the struggle to produce an abundance of material things, surely the citizen will have time for the *pursuit of personal development*. We may expect change at this point. Our curricula of today are not sufficiently culturally oriented. Sputnik has driven the art of homemaking, music, fine arts, arts and crafts, drama, the dance, and even literature into second-rate status. Now as we engage in a worldwide struggle with opportunity to influence many peoples of the world with values associated with the humanities and cultural heritage of Western civilization and particularly the special goals and opportunities America has always held high for every man, we must quickly look to strengthening these aspects of our educational program rather than weakening them.

Furthermore, just when the world sphere of influence is being shifted, the American curricula are meager and barren in the geography, history, and culture of those great and rich areas of India, Japan, South Asia, China, Russia, and the Arab-speaking countries. Likewise, the seething, moving power of central Africa is still the dark continent in our curriculum; but this must not remain so. It is well past the time when we should supplement our curricula content on Western civilization with a large slice of Eastern culture.

The world of the twenty-first century may still use French, Spanish, and German in certain areas, but the mass of communication and transmission of culture will be in English, Russian, Japanese, Arabic, and the major dialects of China, India, and Indonesia. Our schools to date have ignored this great cultural change, and some of our modern language leaders must assume responsibility here. We have here the age-old problem of the vested interest of people with an outmoded professional tool-kit and an unwillingness to get another one. In the future, the world will grow so small and interrelated that under the leadership of America, a common language will be identified, adopted, and used by much of the world. Thus, all major countries, including the United States, will be bilingual—preserving their indigenous or adopted tongue and adding a second. In the meantime, the schools have a national responsibility to develop plans and programs that will provide enough diversity of language learning opportunity that our country will have enough who know the major languages and national cultures to meet the nation's needs as a world power.

Perhaps America's greatest educational shortcoming in preparing people for the twenty-first century is beginning an individual's education too late and stopping it too soon. It has been suggested that a major portion of the problems associated with the unemployed afflicts a child between the ages of two and five. It has been suggested, too, by scholarly researchers, that most children attain 50 percent of their maximum academic attainment by age eight. Thus, we simply can no longer let a significant portion of our opportunity to educate elude us.

Half the jobs now held by Americans did not exist forty years ago. The vocational shifts between 1960 and the year of 2000 will be equally violent. Yet, our educational system gives too little attention to the re-education of the citizen, be he electrician, dentist, bookkeeper, or school board member. It is believed that half the children born this year will be forced to educate themselves vocationally three times before the productive period of their lives is over. Just to preserve the validity of the concept that man can be trusted to govern himself, to make wise choices on problems that vitally affect him and his neighbor, calls for a continuing adult education program that is found in very few communities.

Of course, we must constantly revamp the science program. Obsolescent ideas and scientific data that are no longer true are not helpful—they are dangerous. The social implications of science and technology, and a knowledge and understanding of space will become as essential as geography and must be emphasized. Education must concentrate on teaching *how* to learn. Sources of information, ways to get answers, must become more important to Americans than storing information. Possibly of greatest importance to tomorrow's schools, we must find some way to get more teachers and, in particular, administrators to comprehend how complex, how difficult, how artistic, and yet how scientific good teaching really is. The public is very slow in developing an understanding of the worth and complexity of the teacher's job, and in appropriately recognizing it.

The organization and structure of tomorrow's education will have many innovations. School-district reorganization will go on at an accelerated rate. One-teacher school districts will be eliminated. They will join hands with other districts of like characteristics in sharing teachers, laboratories, building space, and financial resources. State departments will play an ever-increasing role in leadership, research, and consulting services. Children in isolated and sparsely populated sections of the country will be placed in boarding schools. In order to have efficient class groups, whole high school freshmen classes of two or more districts will be combined in one school while all seniors may be sent to another district, the pupils exchanging homes for a few months in order to secure good schooling. The large cities will develop new administrative structures. Schools for 400 will accommodate 600—with one-third of the children learning outside the confines of four walls.

Sometime within the next two decades, we will see a number of colleges and universities with enrollments from 100,000 to 200,000; compulsory education will be extended to approximately age 20 (in great part, this will be an economic decision); and undergraduate colleges and universities will become three-year institutions, with the third year including in it the master's degree. This will become possible because of the emergence of community colleges.

Teachers will be employed on a twelve-month basis, with adequate vacation periods and regularly established periods for curriculum work, research, study, and travel. Schools will be in use more hours each day for both pupils and adults, and the year will be extended to provide many additional opportunities for learning. With more mothers working, with the family changing, school, home, and community agencies will be forced to cooperate more fully and provide many more joint services to children.

Concern for religious training will continue. The end of discussion, debate, and controversy over control or freedom and the support of church-operated schools is not in sight. The exact nature of how a parochial school differs from a public school will be more closely examined. The mounting costs of multiple school systems within a given community will be carefully scrutinized. The need for a force such as the public school to bring about greater cohesiveness and unity will continue to be emphasized. With a greater diversity of religious sects impinging upon life tomorrow, the need for protecting the right to worship as one pleases will become more emphatic. Indeed, the principle of separation of church and state will be more closely guarded by all who value their church and the right to worship in it.

And last, out of the constellation of cultures which is our greatest heritage, will come a rebirth of faith in those concepts that pulled together the great minds who conceived and developed the design of our new nation and gave it life and put it on its feet. Somehow, with a refurbished design in the content of the public-school curriculum, we will develop a great unity among men and at the same time preserve diversity. Independence of thought, independence of choice, independence of philosophical concepts, with the help of teachers who are free to teach and to seek the truth, will fashion and refashion our education as new demands are placed on the individual. With one hand holding fast to our proven heritage of the past and the other stretching eagerly for the exciting future, our thinking citizens and professional leaders will fashion the education of tomorrow which will further man's destiny mightly.

It is time for school administrators especially to begin thinking unthinkable thoughts. We can no longer enjoy the privilege of harboring selfish, vested interests. We must listen to the criticisms hurled at public education (and they seem to come from all quarters). We must weigh each of them carefully, for perhaps there is great truth in the words written by Albert Camus when he said, "Great ideas come into the world as gently as doves. Perhaps, then, if we listen attentively, we shall hear amidst the uproar a faint flutter of wings, the gentle stirring of life and hope."